# CONTENTS

Enjoy A Sna

Off The Rai

This book is sold on the understanding that the publisher and author are not engaged in providing medical, legal or other professional advice or services. The information provided within is for your general knowledge only. The information, advice and strategies contained herein may not suitable for every situation. If you require professional or medical advice or treatment for a specific condition, the services of a competent, qualified professional person should be sought promptly.

This book is designed to provide general information in regard to the subject matter. While reasonable attempts have been made to verify the accuracy of the information provided, neither the author nor the publisher assumes any responsibility for errors, omissions, interpretations or usage of the subject matters within.

Warning on Allergic reactions – some recipes included in this book use nuts or nut oils. These specific recipes should be avoided by:

- anyone with a known nut allergy
- anyone who may be vulnerable to nut allergies such as pregnant and nursing mothers, invalids, the elderly, babies and children

Warning on Eggs – The US Department of Health's advice is that eggs should not be consumed raw. Some recipes included in this book are made with raw or lightly cooked eggs. These specific recipes should be avoided by:

- anyone who may be vulnerable such as pregnant and nursing mothers, invalids, the elderly, babies and children

Warning on Blending Hot Foods and Liquids - Remove from the heat and allow to cool for at least 5 minutes. Carefully transfer to a blender or food processor, ensuring that it is no more than half full. If using a blender, release one corner of the lid, which helps prevent heat explosions. Place a towel over the top of the machine, pulse a few times before processing according to the recipe directions.

# Enjoy A Snack – Without Going Off The Rails!

## Introduction

Whether it's a family gathering during festive holidays such as Thanksgiving, Christmas & New Year or a fun summer-time barbeque, parties can be a time when our healthy-eating good intentions fly out the window. No-one wants to be a party-pooper, constantly saying "no" to what's on offer whilst everyone else tucks in. On the other hand, it's all too easy to over-indulge in high calorie, high-fat snacks and find you've eaten almost a day's worth of calories without even having a meal. Shop-bought processed-food snacks are definitely a danger-zone, as they are often loaded with:

- fat, especially saturated fats or trans fats
- refined sugars
- high levels of salt.

Sadly this can also be true of even traditional home-made party recipes.

The good news is that it doesn't have to be this way! If you crave an indulgent dip, snack or canapé but think they are "off-limits" as part of either a diet or just a healthy-eating regime, think again! You can still enjoy delicious Canapés, Nibbles, Dips, Dippers & Dunkers but all made healthier and lower in fat, such as:

- Red Pepper Caponata Bruschetta
- Caramelised Onion, Apple & Crispy Prosciutto Dip
- Hot & Spicy Roasted Corn & Pepper Dip
- Broad Bean & Basil Spread
- Blooming Onion

The flavoursome recipes in this book are crammed full of delicious, natural, whole food ingredients that taste amazing and make you feel fully satisfied. They are low in calories, low in fat and, importantly, in saturated fat and they don't rely on artificial sweeteners (in fact, they don't use artificial sweeteners at all). With these guilt-free snacks, you enjoy eating any of the above for 85 calories or less, with recipes that are also low in fat and especially low in saturated fat?

## How much to serve?

Deciding how much finger food to serve at a party will depend upon the occasion. If the occasion is nibbles prior to serving a full meal dinner party, then plan to serve 4-5 canapés per person. For a drinks party, allow 8-10 canapés for a shorter event or 10-12 for a longer occasion, and try to stagger serving them rather than having them all out at the start.

With drinks, make sure that there are non-alcoholic choices and drinks suitable for children, if required.

# Ingredient Super Heroes

A healthy balanced diet means eating a diet rich in fruit, vegetables, whole-grain cereals and one that is low in saturated fat and salt. When based on these naturally wholesome ingredients, snacks do not need to be off-limits but rather savoured and enjoyed. So, let's take a look at some of these naturally wholesome, flavour-packed foods that are real snack-recipe super heroes!

## Anchovies

For many people, anchovies are a pizza topping that they may or may not enjoy. However, they are also a superb flavour enhancer. When ground down into a paste and added to recipe, the dish won't taste "fishy" but it will have a wonderfully complex savouriness to it. I prefer anchovy fillets that have been preserved in oil rather than salt, but I always rinse mine then drain them on kitchen towel first of all to remove any excess oil before adding to the recipe.

## Beans & Chickpeas

Beans are naturally low in fat, high in fibre and they can help you feel full to prevent over-eating. In these recipes, I have tended to use ready-cooked tinned beans, as they are wonderfully convenient if you are preparing a number of recipes for a party or gathering, but do make sure that you rinse them in cold water to remove the canning juices before use. However, you can cook your own beans from scratch using dried beans instead, if you prefer. As a general rule of thumb, you will need half the stated quantity of dried beans to ready-cooked, which will need to have been soaked (often overnight) and then must be boiled according to the packet instructions.

## Capers & Caper Berries

The Mediterranean caper bush is the source of two most flavourful but low fat seasoning ingredients; capers, which are actually the flower buds, and it's fruit, which are the larger berries. When cooking I prefer to use tiny nonpareil capers within a dish and save the larger whole caper berries as a garnish. Do make sure that you rinse them before use to remove excess salt or vinegar, and leave them to drain on a piece of kitchen towel.

## Cheese

Whilst cheese is often regarded as a high fat, high calorie ingredient, there are a number of naturally lower fat cheeses available such as ricotta, cottage cheese and fromage frais. Nowadays it's also possible to find reduced fat alternatives of mature hard cheeses such as Cheddar. Other cheeses such as original Stilton and

Parmesan may not be lower in fat, but because they have such a strong flavour, only a little is required to provide that distinctive flavour to a dish or recipe, making little difference to the overall fat and calories content per serving.

## CONDIMENT SAUCES

Although most of my recipes use natural, whole food ingredients, condiment sauces are a useful way to boost flavour too. A dash of Tabasco pepper sauce or a spoonful of soy or sweet chilli sauce can add a tangy piquancy to many snack recipes.

## CORNICHONS (DILL PICKLE)

These French baby gherkins may be small in size but they are big in flavour. They add piquancy as well as crunch to recipes. They should be rinsed then dried on kitchen towel to remove any excess salt before being used in a recipe.

## CRÈME FRAÎCHE AND SOUR CREAM

Reduced fat crème fraîche has over 60% fewer calories and $^2/_3$rds less saturated fat compared to double cream, and reduced fat sour cream is even better at ¾ of the calories and over 80% less saturated fat. With those figures in mind, it's no surprise that these ingredients feature in many of my snack recipes!

## LENTILS

Irrespective of whether they are green, red or Puy lentils, they are naturally low in fat, high in fibre and they can help you feel satisfyingly full. They are a good substitute for minced/ground meat in canapé stuffings or fillings.

## GREEK YOGURT

Low-fat or fat-free Greek yogurt is an absolutely essential ingredient for many healthier versions of traditional dips. It is a great substitute for cream but also can replace oil or mayonnaise too.

## HERBS

Fresh and dried herbs help pack a mighty flavour punch to low-fat recipes. Where possible, try to use fresh herbs. I keep a few pots of the fresh herbs that I use most often on my kitchen window sill. You need to strip off the leaves from herbs such as rosemary and thyme as they have woody stems that are not really edible. However, don't discard the softer stems of herbs such as parsley, coriander (cilantro) or basil – there's tons of flavour in them, they just need to be finely chopped.

## Oil & Fat

Whilst all oils contain the same amount of calories (900 cals per 100g), varieties of oils differ quite considerably in terms of saturated fat. For example, if you swap rapeseed (Canola) oil for olive oil, you'll reduce the saturated fat by over 50%. Using an oil misting spray instead of liquid oil can also help to significantly reduce the quantity of oil used in a recipe or dish.

## Olives

Where you aware that like the tomato, an olive is actually a fruit not a vegetable? Higher in fat and calories than many other fruits (or vegetables for that matter), used sparingly in a recipe they will add complexity and flavour.

## Roasted Garlic

If you haven't yet tried roasting garlic, you are in for an epiphany, even if you think you don't like garlic! Roasted garlic is much milder than its raw version and has none of its harshness. You can spread the roasted garlic paste directly onto bread or crackers in place of butter, or use it as a seasoning to add depth of flavour to dishes.

## Roasted Red Peppers

As with garlic, roasting peppers mellows their flavour and also allows you to remove their skin, which some people find hard to digest. You can buy jars of ready-roasted peppers, just be sure to rinse them before use, especially if they have been stored in oil or brine. Lay on kitchen towel to dry.

## Seeds

Whilst seeds are relatively high in calories, they are a great source of good fats and they are generally about 10-15% lower in calories than nuts. Their protein and fibre content can also help with feeling full. Also, a small amount of tiny seeds such as poppy seeds and sesame seeds can go a long way in providing a satisfyingly crunchy topping without lots of extra calories.

## Spices

Spices can really help dial up the flavour and not just the heat in snack recipes, and many can be used in both sweet and savoury dishes (think cinnamon, ginger, nutmeg and star anise). Whole spices retain more of their flavour when stored, but ready ground spices are convenient and quick. However, both black pepper and nutmeg really should be freshly ground (pepper) or grated (nutmeg) and it's worth the faff to do so.

# KITCHENWARE & EQUIPMENT FOR HEALTHIER COOKING

The good news is that you do not need a whole host of fancy equipment to make the recipes in this cookbook (or any of my cookbooks for that matter). However, I do find the following items to be particularly useful.

## Measuring/Weighing Tools

Proper measuring and weighing can really make a difference to reducing both calories and fat. Accurate ingredient quantities are key to ensuring that the recipes in this cookbook remain low fat and low calories. So, the following will really help with accuracy:

- a standard set of measuring spoons: 1/8th tsp to 1 tbsp
- a standard set of cup measures: ¼ cup, 1/3 cup, 1/2 cup, 1 cup
- a set of digital kitchen scales
- a small measuring jug

## Non-stick Wok or Chef's Sauté Pan

Without doubt, I find a good quality non-stick Chef's Sauté Pan the most versatile and useful type of pan to have to hand in the kitchen for healthier, low fat cooking.

## Non-Stick Baking Trays

One with a shallow rim will be the most versatile.

## Mini Food Processor

A mini-food processor is a really useful addition to any kitchen but especially so when you are preparing snacks. As well as being perfectly suited to food processing smaller quantities such salsa, its smaller bowl size makes it ideal to mince herbs and garlic, blend flavouring pastes or grind toasted whole spices. Do choose a mini food processor though not a mini chopper, as these are only really suitable for the latter tasks listed. A mini food processor needs a bowl capacity of around a 1 litre/quart with a liquid blending capacity of around 500ml/2 cups.

# How to Use This Cookbook

## American Vs Metric Measurements & Ingredients

All recipes are provided in both Metric and American measurements. In order to provide meaningful equivalents, there may be slight "rounding" differences between the two systems, but these do not make a material difference to the overall calorie count. However, please follow either the metric or American measures within a recipe, don't mix the two together.

To make this cookbook easy to use, both UK English and American English names have been given for ingredients where they differ in common usage, for example, courgette or zucchini.

The description of egg sizes also differ between the UK and the US. However, each recipe clearly states the both the UK and US egg size required for the recipe.

Standard level spoon measurements are used in all recipes:

- 1 tsp = 5ml
- 1 tbsp = 15ml
- A pinch = $^1/_8$ tsp

## Vegetarian Recipes & Vegetarian Options

Recipes suitable for Vegetarians are indicated with the V symbol or the Ve symbol if they are also Vegan.

V – Vegetarian meaning no meat, poultry, game, fish or shellfish, nor any by-product from processing such ingredients. However, Vegetarian recipes may include honey, eggs and dairy. Where a recipe includes cheese but is indicated with a (V) symbol, it assumes that the cook will use vegetarian cheese if that is required.

Ve – Vegan meaning no meat, poultry, game, fish, shellfish, dairy, honey, eggs nor by-product from processing such ingredients.

Also, if a recipe does include one of two ingredients that preclude it from being either vegetarian or vegan, where possible, I will include alternative options showing how the recipe can be adapted, for example, non-dairy margarine for butter. Old hands at recipe adapting will already be very familiar with this, so apologies in advance for some fairly obvious substitutions. However, my cook books are bought by a wide variety of readers, but I've included this advice especially if you do not regularly cook for these dietary needs and are not used to making such recipe substitutions.

# Further Resources

## More Low Fat Cookbooks

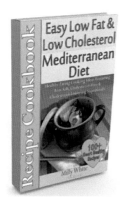  

If you have enjoyed the recipes in this cookbook, you may also be interested in further books by Milly White:

*Easy Low Fat & Low Cholesterol Mediterranean Diet Cookbook,* watch a video preview on Youtube @ https://youtu.be/F1z-XMF84qI

*Healthy Brunch & Breakfast Eats Low Fat & Low Cholesterol Recipe Cookbook,* watch a video preview on Youtube @ https://youtu.be/ke9A11qaPcc

*Quick & Easy Low Calorie & Low Fat Desserts, Cakes & Bakes Diet Recipe Cookbook.*

*Discover more about these books on page*

## Bonus Two-Day 5:2 Diet Plan FREE Giveaway

As a special Thank You to my readers, I have available an exclusive & free special bonus: FREE 1 Day Taster eBook, my complete and easy step-by-step guide to the 5:2 diet. Download your free copy here https://Free52DietRecipes.blogspot.co.uk

# STAYING CONNECTED

Please do also take a look at my author blog, MillyWhiteCooks.com.

As well as details on my full range of cookbooks, you will also find articles and helpful information on:

- Ingredients
- Cooking Techniques
- Equipment
- Health News
- Nutrition Information
- Special Offers

You can find me on social media too:

 MillyWhiteCooks.com     facebook.com/MillyWhiteCooks

 pinterest.com/MillyWhiteCooks    instagram.com/MillyWhiteCooks

twitter.com/MillyWhiteCooks    plus.google.com/+MillywhitecooksBooks/posts

## Red Pepper Caponata Bruschetta (V)

Makes: 30     Ready In: 35 mins

Each: 44 cals ~ 1g Total Fat ~ 0.1g Sat Fat ~ 7g Carbs ~ 1g Fibre ~ 1g Protein

Ingredients

- 3 red bell peppers
- 2 medium tomatoes
- 1 tbsp Nonpareille capers
- 2 garlic cloves, divided
- 1 tsp tomato purée
- 1-2 dashes Tabasco sauce
- 300g (10½ oz) French baguette bread
- ½ tsp freshly ground black pepper
- Frylight olive oil spray

- 1 red onion
- 30 pitted black olives
- 3 tbsp red wine vinegar
- ½ tsp dried red chilli flakes
- 1 tsp brown sugar
- small bunch fresh parsley
- 1 tbsp rapeseed oil
- ¼ tsp sea (kosher) salt

## Directions

Preheat the oven to 180C fan, 400F, Gas Mark 6 and place 2 shallow baking sheets into warm.

Slice the French stick into 30 thin slices. Cut the garlic cloves in half lengthwise. Remove the baking sheets from the oven and add the rapeseed oil, spreading it across the surface. Lay out the bread slices evenly across the baking sheets, lightly pressing them into the oiled surface. Turn them over and rub them with the cut sides of the ½ garlic cloves. Sprinkle over with black pepper. Make space and place the red peppers on the baking sheets too (but make sure they are not too close to the bread slices, otherwise place the peppers into a separate baking dish).

Return the baking sheets to the oven. After 5 mins, take them out and turn over the bread slices over then return to the oven for a further 5-8mins until golden brown and crispy. Remove the bread slices from the baking sheets to a wire rack to cool but return the red peppers to the oven to roast for a further 10-15 mins until the skins are charred. Remove from the oven, place into a bowl and cover with kitchen film. Set aside to steam and cool.

Meanwhile, finely mince the garlic cloves. Peel the red onion, cut in half from top to bottom and thinly slice. Heat a non-stick sauté pan over a medium heat and spritz 4 times with Frylight spray. Add the onions and sauté for 10 mins until softened and lightly golden. Whilst the onions sauté, place the tomatoes in heat-proof bowl and cover with boiling water. After 1 min, remove the tomatoes with a slotted spoon and, when they are cooled enough to handle, slip off the skins and discard. Dice the tomato flesh. When the onions are golden, add the minced garlic and chilli flakes and sauté for 1 min. Add the diced tomatoes and tomato purée and cook for a further 2 mins, then add the sugar, salt, Tabasco and vinegar. Toss well to combine and cook for a further 3 mins. Set aside to cool.

Rinse and drain the capers and olives, dry on kitchen towel then roughly chop. Remove all the pith, seeds and skin from the cooled roasted peppers and cut the flesh into strips. Stir these vegetables into the cooled tomato and onion mixture and check the seasoning.

Mince the parsley and stir $^2/_3$rds into the cooled pepper caponata. Spoon the caponata evenly over the brushetta slices and sprinkle them with the remaining chopped parsley.

Make Ahead Tip: Cook the caponata and brushetta 2-3 days in advance. Store the caponata in a sealable food container in the fridge, and the brushetta in an airtight container.

# DEVILISH EGGS (V)

Makes: 12 halves  Ready In: 35 mins

Each: 46 cals ~ 2g Total Fat ~ 0.7g Sat Fat ~ 2g Carbs ~ 1g Fibre ~ 4g Protein

Ingredients

- 6 UK medium (US large) free range eggs
- 120g (¾ cup) tinned cooked chickpeas
- 2 celery stalks
- 1 tsp white wine vinegar
- ½ tsp mustard powder
- 2 dashes Tabasco sauce
- ¼ tsp sea (kosher) salt
- 1 tbsp Nonpareille Capers (fine baby capers) in brine
- 1 tsp smoked paprika

Directions

Put the eggs into a saucepan that's large enough to hold them in a single layer and add enough cold water to cover them by about 1.5cm/½". Place over a medium heat and bring the water to a boil then turn down to a gentle simmer and cook for a further 7 minutes. Drain immediately, rinse under running cold water for 1 minute and pop them into a bowl for cold water for a further 5 mins.

Meanwhile, de-thread the celery stalks by running a vegetable peeler over the ribbed side to remove the strings. Finely dice the celery. Put the rinsed and drained chickpeas into a food processor along with the vinegar, salt, mustard powder and Tabasco sauce. Purée until smooth.

Drain the eggs and peel off the shells. Pat the eggs dry on kitchen paper. Carefully cut each egg in half lengthwise. It helps to keep wiping your knife clean between each egg. Scoop out the egg yolks and add the yolks from 4 of the eggs to the food processor (discarding the remaining 2 yolks). Pulse the processor until the mixture is well combined. Finally, add the diced celery and pulse once or twice (you don't want to purée the celery, just fold it into the eggy mixture).

Arrange the egg whites onto a serving plate. Use a teaspoon to evenly divide the filling between the whites, then lightly dust the filled eggs with smoked paprika. Finally, scatter 2-3 baby capers over each egg half.

Make Ahead Tip: These can be made up to a day in advance and stored in the fridge in a sealed container.

# Maple Spiced Chickpeas & Seeds (V, Ve)

Serves: 18      Ready In: 30-45 mins

Per tbsp: 61 cals ~ 2g Total Fat ~ 0.3g Sat Fat ~ 7g Carbs ~ 2g Fibre ~ 3g Protein

## Ingredients

- 400g (2 cups) cooked chickpeas
- 40g ($^1/_3$ cup) pumpkin seeds
- 35g (¼ cup) sunflower seeds
- 1 tbsp sunflower oil
- 2 tbsp + 2 tsp maple syrup, divided
- 1¼ tsp ground cinnamon
- ½ tsp mixed spice
- ¼ tsp Chinese 5 spice mix

## Directions

Preheat the oven 140C fan, 325F, Gas Mark 3.

Rinse the chickpeas and drain, then spread out onto a double layer of kitchen towel and pat to dry completely.

Line the baking sheet with baking parchment. Spread out the chickpeas and seeds over the sheet. In a small jug, add the oil, followed by half the maple syrup and the spices, and whisk together with a fork. Drizzle over the chickpeas and seeds, then tossing them thoroughly in the spicy coating and spread out again into a single layer.

Place into the oven for 10mins, then remove from the oven and drizzle over the remaining maple syrup. Toss again and spread out. Return to the oven and check the chickpeas after 5 mins, roast for a further 5 mins only if required. Remove from the oven, toss again then allow to cool for a few minutes before serving warm or completely cool to serve cold latter.

Store & Keep Tip: Transfer the completely cold chickpeas to sterilised airtight glass jars or seal in cellophane treat bags to keep for up to a month.

# Chocolate Almond Star Cookies (V)

Makes: 38        Ready In: 30 mins + resting time

Each: 49 cals ~ 3g Total Fat ~ 0.8g Sat Fat ~ 5g Carbs ~ 1g Fibre ~ 1g Protein

Ingredients

- 1 UK medium (US large) free range egg white
- 110g (1 cup) ground almonds
- ½ tbsp milled flaxseeds
- 165g (¾ cup) natural caster (superfine) sugar
- 85g (½ cup) finely chopped plain dark (bittersweet) chocolate
- ¾ tsp ground cinnamon
- ¼ tsp mixed spice
- 2 tsp icing (powdered) sugar, optional

Equipment

- 1x baking sheet
- baking parchment
- star cookie cutter

## Directions

Break up the chocolate and place into a food processor, whiz until finely grated. Add the ground almonds, sugar, flaxseeds and spices and pulse until well combined and a fine texture. Finally, tip in the egg white and pulse until the dough has come together (it will be quite a "crumbly" dough).

Layout a large piece of parchment paper on your work surface and transfer the dough to the paper. Knead together and then pat out. Lay another sheet of over the top and toll-out the dough to $^1/_3$cm/$^1/_8$" thick (about the thickness of a £ coin or 2xcent coins). Run a palette knife under the dough to loosen it then use a star cookie cutter to cut out shapes, transferring to baking sheets lined with baking parchment. Re-roll the scraps and repeat, using the last few scraps to make 2-3 thumb-print cookies (roll into a small ball and just press with your thumb to flatten). Cover the cut cookies with clean kitchen towels and allow the shapes to dry for 3 hrs.

Preheat the oven to 140C Fan, 325F, Gas Mark 3.

Remove the cloth covers and transfer the baking sheets to the oven. Bake until lightly puffed (about 12-15 mins). Remove from the oven and lightly dust with icing sugar. Allow to cool for 10 mins on the baking sheets then transfer to a wire rack. These are absolutely delicious served whilst still warm.

Store & Keep Tip: Transfer the cookies to an airtight container (with a sheet of baking parchment between each layer) to keep for up to a week.

Want to Freeze These? Alternatively, prepare and cut out the cookies but don't bake them. Instead, place them on a suitably sized baking sheet straight into the freezer and freeze uncovered for 2 hrs. Once frozen through, either cover the tray in kitchen foil to seal or remove the cookies from the tray and place in a single layer into freezer bags or container. To bake, remove the quantity that you need from the freezer about 1 hr before cooking (or overnight) and place back onto a lined baking sheet to defrost, then bake as above.

# Ricotta Stuffed Apricots (V)

Makes: 30     Ready In: 15 mins + 1 hr chilling time

Each: 29 cals ~ 1g Total Fat ~ 0.2g Sat Fat ~ 4g Carbs ~ 1g Fibre ~ 1g Protein

## Ingredients

- 60g (½ cup) Ricotta cheese
- 35g (¼ cup) blanched hazelnuts
- 30g (¼ cup) dried cranberries
- 2 tsp icing (powdered) sugar
- 1 tbsp Amaretto liqueur
- 30 whole ready-to-eat dried apricots (about 210g/ 1$^2/_3$ cups)

## Directions

Chop the hazelnuts into small pieces. Heat a non-stick sauté pan over a medium heat and add the chopped nuts. Toast the hazelnuts until lightly golden, keeping a close watch and stirring to make sure they don't burn. As soon as the nuts are toasted, remove from the pan to saucer to prevent further cooking and to allow to cool.

Meanwhile, use a sharp knife to split the apricots $^2/_3$rds open. In a small bowl, whisk together the ricotta cheese, sugar and Amaretto. Roughly chop the cranberries and add these to the bowl. Set aside 4 tsp of toasted hazelnuts for decoration and add the remainder to the bowl. Beat the cheese mix until thoroughly combined.

Use a teaspoon to stuff each apricot with 1 tsp of cheese mixture, then dip the cheese edge into the retained chopped nuts. Place the stuffed apricots onto a serving plate, cover with kitchen film and pop into the fridge for 1 hr before serving (can be made up to 4 hrs before serving).

Make this Nut-free? Replace the hazelnuts with toasted sesame seeds.

Make Ahead Tip: These can be made up to a day in advance and stored in the fridge covered in kitchen film.

# Strawberry Cheesecake Bites (V)

Makes: 36     Ready In: 15 mins + 1 hr chilling time

Each: 15 cals ~ 1g Total Fat ~ 0.6g Sat Fat ~ 1g Carbs ~ 0g Fibre ~ 0g Protein

## Ingredients

- 36 medium sized fresh strawberries
- 155g (1¼ cups) Ricotta cheese
- 60ml (¼ cup) whipping (heavy) cream
- 25g (3½ tbsp) icing (powdered) sugar
- 1 vanilla pod
- 1½ reduced fat digestive biscuits (graham crackers)

## Directions

Place the cream into the bowl and whisk into stiff peaks. Split the vanilla pod in half lengthwise and scrap out the seeds, add these to the bowl along with the ricotta cheese. Sift in the sugar and then beat together to combine. Pop into the fridge to chill and firm up.

Meanwhile, use a sharp knife to hull the strawberries then use a melon baller to carefully hollow out a space in each berry. Put the biscuit into a freezer bag and use a rolling pin to crush it into fine crumbs.

Transfer the chilled cheesecake filling into a piping bag fitted with a round nozzle and pipe the filling into the strawberries, and sprinkle them with the biscuit crumbs. Place onto a serving plate and serve immediately.

# Mini Fruit Skewers With Honey Yogurt Dip (V)

Serves: 12     Ready In: 10 mins

Per Serving of 3: 42 cals ~ 0g Total Fat ~ 0.0g Sat Fat ~ 7g Carbs ~ 1g Fibre ~ 2g Protein

## Ingredients

- 36 small strawberries
- 180g (²/₃ cup) 0% Greek yogurt
- 1 tbsp pure honey
- 36 green grapes
- 9 fresh figs
- 36 mini bamboo skewers

## Directions

In a small bowl, whisk together the yogurt and honey.

Cut the figs into quarters. Thread each skewer with a fig quarter, followed by a strawberry then a grape. Serve the skewers with the dipping sauce on the side.

# Duck Satay Skewers

Makes: 30    Ready In: 30 mins + marinating time

Each: 15 cals ~ 1g Total Fat ~ 0.1g Sat Fat ~ 1g Carbs ~ 0g Fibre ~ 2g Protein

Ingredients

- 30 baby corn
- 30 chestnut mushrooms
- 175g (6 oz) skinless duck breast
- 2 garlic cloves
- 1 tbsp finely grated fresh ginger root
- 1 tsp Chinese five spice
- 4 tsp no added fat or salt peanut butter
- 60ml 0% Greek yogurt
- 2 tbsp reduced salt soy sauce, divided
- Frylight olive oil spray
- 30 bamboo skewers, soaked in water

Directions

Finely grate the ginger and garlic into a bowl. Add 4 tsp soy sauce and the Chinese 5 spice and whisk together. Remove any skin and all visible fat from the breast and cut into 30 strips, then cut each strip into half. Add to the marinade, toss well to combine & set aside for 30 mins. Place the skewers into a dish of cold water to soak.

Meanwhile, in a ramekin, whisk together the yogurt, peanut butter and 2 tsp soy sauce. Cover and chill in the fridge until required.

Preheat the oven to 20C fan, 425F, Gas Mark 7.

Place a non-stick baking sheet in to warm. Assemble the satay skewers. Cut the baby corn and mushrooms in half. Thread each skewer twice with a skewer a piece of corn, duck then a half mushroom. Repeat with the remaining skewers. Remove the baking sheet from the oven and spritz with 3 sprays of Frylight olive oil mist. Lay the skewers on the sheet and spritz again with Frylight and brush over any remaining marinade. Return the baking sheet to the oven and cook for 12-15 mins, turning the skewers over half way through.

Serve the duck skewers with the satay dipping sauce on the side.

Make Ahead Tips: The duck can be prepared and marinated up to 24hrs in advance and stored, covered, in the fridge. The dipping sauce can also be made up to 24hrs in advance and stored, covered, in the fridge.

# Boozy Devils on Horseback

Makes: 30      Ready In: 15 mins + 1 hr chilling time

Each: 25 cals ~ 0g Total Fat ~ 0.1g Sat Fat ~ 4g Carbs ~ 0g Fibre ~ 1g Protein

## Ingredients

- 10 slices Prosciutto ham, all visible fat removed
- 5 tbsp Mango chutney (or any homemade chutney)
- 2 tbsp Cognac or Brandy
- 30 whole stoned ready-to-eat dried prunes (about 210g/ 1²/₃ cups)
- 30 cocktail sticks

## Directions

Make sure that the prunes have no stones and put into a bowl. Pour over the cognac/brandy and stir. Cover with a clean cloth and set aside to soak for at least an hour (and you could leave it overnight). Soak 30 wooden cocktail sticks in a bowl of water.

Preheat the oven to 180C Fan, 400F, Gas Mark 6.

Once the prunes have soaked, take the Prosciutto slices and cut each lengthwise into 3 strip. Take a prune and stuff it with ½ tsp of chutney, then place it at the end of one of the strips and roll-it up. Secure with a soaked cocktail stick and place onto a baking sheet. Once all the prunes are stuffed and wrapped, pop the backing sheet into the oven. Roast for 13-15 mins until the ham is crispy. Allow to cool for 2-3 mins before serving.

Make Ahead Tip: These can be made up to a day in advance and stored in the fridge in a sealed container before cooking.

# Bloody Mary Mini Muffins (V)

Makes: 12     Ready In: 45 mins

Each: 56 cals ~ 1g Total Fat ~ 0.4g Sat Fat ~ 8g Carbs ~ 1g Fibre ~ 2g Protein

## Ingredients

- 35g (¼ cup) wholemeal flour
- 10 sun-dried tomatoes (not in oil)
- 2 celery heart sticks, divided
- 75ml (5 tbsp) buttermilk
- 1 tsp lime juice
- 1 tsp Worcestershire Sauce
- 1 UK medium (US large) free range egg
- ¼ tsp bicarbonate of soda
- ¼ tsp sea (kosher) salt
- Dusting cayenne pepper, for decoration
- 65g(½ cup) maize meal
- 1 clove garlic
- 2 spring onions (scallions)
- 1 tsp rapeseed oil
- 2 tsp tomato purée
- ½ tsp Tabasco sauce
- 4 tbsp Ricotta cheese
- ½ tsp baking powder
- ¼ tsp black pepper
- 12 hole mini muffin pan

## Directions

Preheat the oven 180C, 400F, Gas Mark 6. Line a muffin tin with 12 paper mini muffin cases.

De-thread 1 of the sticks of celery by running a vegetable peeler over the ribbed side of the celery to remove the "strings", set aside the other stick. Finely dice the de-threaded celery along with the sun-dried tomatoes. Finely slice the spring onions/scallions. Mix the onions, tomatoes and diced celery together. Very finely mince or grate the garlic clove.

In a jug, whisk together the buttermilk, egg, rapeseed oil, tomato purée, lime juice and Tabasco. Sift the flours, baking powder and soda, spices, salt and black pepper into a roomy bowl and mix together to combine. Make a well in the centre of the dry ingredients, pour in the wet ingredients. Set aside 2 tbsps of the celery/onion/tomato mix then add the remainder to the bowl along with the minced garlic. Beat the mixture into a batter.

Spoon the batter evenly into prepared muffin wrappers, and top each muffin with ½ tsp of the reserved diced vegetables. Bake for 8-10 mins until golden brown and when a toothpick inserted into the centre of the muffins comes out clean. Remove from the oven, cool in the tin for 10 mins, then transfer to cool onto wire racks.

Meanwhile, cut the reserved celery stick into 24 small batons. Once the muffins have cooled, top each one with 1 tsp ricotta cheese and decorate with 2 celery batons and a very light dusting of cayenne pepper.

Store & Keep Tip: Once cooled, store in an airtight container & eat within 2 days.

Want to Freeze These? Prepare the muffins completely but instead of putting in the oven, place them in the muffin tin straight into the freezer and freeze uncovered for 2 hrs. Once frozen through, remove the muffins in their cases from the tray and place in a single layer into container. To bake, remove the quantity that you need from the freezer about 1 hr before cooking (or overnight) and place back into the mini muffin tin to defrost, then follow the instructions above for baking.

## Spinach & Parmesan Mushroom Bites (V)

Makes: 30      Ready In: 20 mins

Each: 10 cals ~ 0g Total Fat ~ 0.2g Sat Fat ~ 0g Carbs ~ 0g Fibre ~ 1g Protein

### Ingredients

- 30 medium chestnut mushrooms
- 125g (¾ cup) frozen spinach, defrosted
- 75g ($^1/_3$ cup) 3% fat soft cheese
- 3 tbsp finely grated parmesan cheese, divided
- 3 garlic cloves
- 1½ tsp dried herbs de Provence
- ¼ tsp freshly grated nutmeg
- ¼ tsp freshly ground black pepper
- 4 sprays Frylight olive oil spray
- ¼ tsp sea (kosher) salt

### Directions

Preheat the oven to 180C fan, 400F, Gas Mark 6 and place an oven-proof sauté pan in to warm.

Wipe the mushrooms clean and carefully remove the stalks. Finely chop the stalks, and mince the garlic cloves. Squeeze any excess water from the defrosted, drained spinach and chop. Add this to a bowl, along with the soft cheese and 2 tbsp of parmesan (set aside the remainder for later). Add the chopped mushrooms stalks, garlic, dried herbs, nutmeg, salt and pepper. Beat well to combine.

Turn the mushrooms open side down on a chopping board and spritz with Frylight. Turn back over and spoon the filling evenly between the mushrooms. Sprinkle each stuffed mushroom with a little of the reserved parmesan cheese. Remove the warmed sauté pan from the oven and add the mushrooms. Return to the oven and back for 15 mins until tender. Serve hot, warm or cold.

Make Ahead Tips: The mushrooms can be fully prepared up to 24hrs in advance and stored in the fridge. Cook according to the above instructions, but for 18mins.

# Tomato & Spinach Crustless Mini Quiches (V)

Makes: 12     Ready In: 25 mins

Each: 28 cals ~ 2g Total Fat ~ 0.7g Sat Fat ~ 1g Carbs ~ 0g Fibre ~ 3g Protein

## Ingredients

- 100g ($^2/_3$ cup) frozen spinach, defrosted
- 6 cherry tomatoes
- 2 UK medium (US large) free range eggs
- 60g (4 tbsp) 3% fat soft cheese
- 2 tbsp finely grated parmesan cheese
- 4 sprays Frylight olive oil spray
- pinch freshly grated nutmeg
- ½ tsp dried oregano
- $^1/_8$ tsp sea (kosher) salt
- ¼ tsp freshly ground black pepper

## Directions

Preheat the oven to 160C Fan, 350F, Gas Mark 4.

Defrost and drain the frozen spinach then squeeze out as much of the moisture as possible and chop. Slice the cherry tomatoes in half.

Put the soft cheese in a bowl and add finely grated Parmesan cheese and mix together, then whisk in the eggs, one at a time. Fold in the drained, squeezed spinach and dried oregano and season with salt, pepper and freshly grated nutmeg.

Spray a non-stick 12-hole mini muffin pan with Frylight olive oil spray. Spoon the egg mixture evenly into the pan, and top each one with a half cherry tomato. Place into the oven for 12-15 mins until the quiches are golden and set. Remove from the oven and allow to cool for 5 mins in the pan.

They can be served warm or cold.

Make Ahead Tip: Once cooled, store in an airtight container in the fridge up to 2 days before serving. The mini quiches can be re-warmed in the oven for 4-5 mins before serving.

# Mediterranean Mini Scones (V)

Makes: 30      Ready In: 25 mins

Each: 52 cals ~ 2g Total Fat ~ 0.5g Sat Fat ~ 6g Carbs ~ 1g Fibre ~ 2g Protein

## Ingredients

- 260g (2 cups) wholemeal (whole wheat) flour
- ½ tbsp bicarbonate of soda (baking soda)
- 40g (2¾ tbsp) sunflower spread, very well chilled
- 6 sun-dried tomatoes (not in oil)
- 1 UK medium (US large) free range egg
- 150ml (½ cup + 2 tbsp) buttermilk
- 75g (½ cup) crumbled lighter (12% fat) feta cheese
- 1 tbsp baking powder
- 1 tbsp olive oil
- 8 black olives
- 1 tsp herbs de Provence

## Directions

Preheat the oven 180C Fan, 400F, Gas Mark 6. Line a baking sheet with baking parchment.

In a large bowl, whisk together the flour, dried herbs, soda and baking powder. Add the sunflower spread and use your fingertips to rub it into the flour until it resembles fine breadcrumbs. Finely chop the olives and sun-dried tomatoes and crumble the feta cheese. Stir all of these into the mixture. Crack the egg into a small jug, beat lightly, add the buttermilk and whisk again. Make a well in the centre of the flour mix, pour in the olive oil, followed by about ²/₃ of the egg and buttermilk mixture. Bring together with a round-bladed knife to form a soft dough (you may need another spoon or 2 of buttermilk if the mixture is too dry).

Tip the dough onto a lightly floured work surface, knead briefly until smooth then roll it out to 2cm thick. Using a 3cm (1.25") round cutter, cut out 30 mini scones, re-rolling the dough as you go.

Transfer the scones on the prepared baking sheet, making sure they are well spaced. Brush the tops with a little extra egg/buttermilk. Bake for 10-12 mins until well risen and golden. Transfer to a rack to cool.

Store & Keep Tip: Once cooled, store in an airtight container and eat within 2 days.

Want to Freeze These? Once the scones are cut out and brushed with the buttermilk, transfer to the freezer and freeze uncovered for 2 hrs. Once frozen through, place in a single layer into container. To bake, remove the quantity that you need from the freezer about 1 hr before cooking (or overnight) then follow the instructions above for baking.

# Balsamic Basil Tomatoes on Toast (V)

Makes: 30      Ready In: 30 mins + marinating time

Each: 42 cals ~ 1g Total Fat ~ 0.1g Sat Fat ~ 7g Carbs ~ 1g Fibre ~ 1g Protein

Ingredients

- 30 medium tomatoes
- 3 tbsp balsamic vinegar
- 4 garlic cloves
- 2 tsp dried herbs de Provence
- 30 fresh basil leaves
- 300g (10½ oz) French baguette bread
- 1½ tsp freshly ground black pepper, divided
- ¼ tsp sea (kosher) salt
- 1 tbsp rapeseed oil

## Directions

Preheat the oven to 180C fan, 400F, Gas Mark 6 & warm 2-3 shallow baking sheets

Place the peeled garlic cloves and sea (kosher) salt into a pestle and mortar, if you have one. Grind these together to form a paste. If you don't have a pestle and mortar, pop the garlic and salt onto a chopping board and simply use the flat side of a kitchen knife to work together into a paste and then transfer to a small bowl. Add the vinegar, dried herbs and ½ tsp black pepper and whisk together.

Cut the tomatoes in half. Slice the French stick into 30 thin slices.

Remove 1 of the baking sheets from the oven and place the tomatoes onto it, cut sides up. Spoon over the vinaigrette dressing and place a basil leaf on top. Return the sheet to the oven and cook for 15-20 mins until the tomatoes are softened.

After 5 mins, take out the other baking sheet(s) and add the rapeseed oil, spreading it across the surface. Lay out the bread slices evenly across the baking sheets, lightly pressing them into the oiled surface. Turn them over and sprinkle over with black pepper. Return to the oven. After 5 mins, take them out and turn the slices over then return to the oven for a further 5-8mins until golden brown and crispy.

Transfer the toasted bread slices to platters, peppered side up, and top each on with a roasted tomato half. These can be served hot, warm or cold.

Make Ahead Tip: Cook the tomatoes and toasts 2-3 days in advance. Store the tomatoes in a sealable food container in the fridge, and the toasts in an airtight container. To serve, assemble the tomatoes on the toast and serve cold or re-warm in the oven for 5 mins.

# Beetroot & Horseradish Crostini (V)

Makes: 24     Ready In: 50mins

Each: 37 cals ~ 1g Total Fat ~ 0.2g Sat Fat ~ 6g Carbs ~ 0g Fibre ~ 1g Protein

## Ingredients

- 3 medium raw beetroots
- 1 tbsp redcurrant jelly/sauce
- 1 tbsp grated fresh ginger root
- 3 tbsp half fat crème fraîche
- ½ tsp freshly ground black pepper
- Frylight olive oil spray

- 1 orange
- 1 tsp rapeseed (canola) oil
- 1 tbsp creamed horseradish
- 200g (7 oz) mini baguette
- ¼ tsp salt
- small bunch fresh parsley

## Directions

Preheat the oven to 180C fan, 400F, Gas Mark 6. Put a baking sheet and roasting dish into the oven to warm.

Cut the baguette into 24 thin slices. Finely zest the peel of the orange into a bowl, then squeeze in its juice. Add the grated fresh ginger, redcurrant jelly, rapeseed oil, salt and. Whisk well to combine. Trim the tops and tails off the beetroot, then thinly peel off the skins with a vegetable peeler (it's best to wear rubber gloves when doing this). Cut the roots into small dice and toss them in the marinade.

Remove the baking sheet and roasting dish from the oven. Lay the bread slices out onto the baking sheet and spritz 3-4 times with Frylight spray. Turn them over and spray again. Pour the marinated beetroot into the warm dish, cover with foil.

Return both the baking sheet and roasting dish to the oven. After 7 mins, remove the baking sheet and turn the bread slices over. Return to the oven and cook for a further 5 mins until golden and crispy, then remove from the oven along with the roasting dish. Give the beetroot dice a good toss then return to the oven without the foil for a further 10-15mins until they are completely tender.

Meanwhile, whisk together the horseradish and crème fraîche. Chill in the fridge.

Once cooked, remove the beetroot from the oven and allow to cool slightly until warm rather than steaming hot. Set aside 24 parsley leaves then finely mince the remainder. Stir through the cooked beetroot.

Assemble the crostini by placing onto a serving plate. Divide the warm beetroot over the crostini and top each one with ½ tsp of horseradish cream and a parsley leaf.

# Mini Bubble & Squeak Cakes with Roasted Tomatoes (V)

Makes: 36          Ready In: 55mins

Each: 38 cals ~ 1g Total Fat ~ 0.1g Sat Fat ~ 7g Carbs ~ 1g Fibre ~ 1g Protein

## Ingredients

- 7 medium red potatoes
- 18 cherry tomatoes
- 2 tbsp sour cream
- 3 tbsp cornflour (corn starch)
- 3 tbsp Worcestershire Sauce
- ½ tsp freshly ground black pepper
- 30 Brussels sprouts
- 2 tsp rapeseed oil
- 1 tbsp sunflower spread
- 18 cherry tomatoes
- freshly grated nutmeg
- ½ tsp salt, divided

## Directions

Trim the Brussels sprouts and remove any tough outer leaves. Cut in half. Peel and quarter the potatoes. Bring a pan of water to the boil and add ¼ tsp salt. Add the sprouts, return to the boil and simmer for 4 mins until tender but with a little bite still. Use a slotted spoon to remove the sprouts to a sieve (leaving the water in the pan) and run them under cold water to refresh. Leave to drain. Add the potatoes to the saucepan and bring in back to the boil. Simmer for about 15mins until tender.

Meanwhile, once the sprouts are drained and cool enough to handle, finely shred them. When the potatoes are tender, drain them and then return them to the pan. Replace the lid and allow the cooked potatoes to steam for a further 3mins.

Preheat the oven to 170C Fan, 375F, Gas Mark 5. Add the rapeseed oil to a shallow-sided roasting tray and put into the oven to heat up

Mash the potatoes with a masher and beat in the remaining ¼ tsp salt, sour cream, sunflower spread, black pepper and a pinch of freshly grated nutmeg. Add the shredded sprouts to the mash and beat to combine, and allow to cool slightly.

Spread the cornflour/corn starch onto a plate. When the mash is cool enough to handle, form 36 balls of mixture then flatten with your hand into round patties. Lightly dust the cakes with the cornflour/corn starch, shake off any excess.

Take the roasting tray out of the oven and make sure that the oil is spread out evenly across all of the base. Spread the patties out onto the tray and pop into the oven. Meanwhile, slice the cherry tomatoes in half. After 12 mins, remove the baking tray from the oven and turn over all of the patties. Place a ½ tomato on top of each cake and spoon over ¼ tsp Worcestershire sauce. Return to the oven and bake for a further 13-15 mins, until the cakes are golden and crispy on the outside, and the tomatoes are cooked and softened.

# Crunchy Asian Beef & Radish Gem Lettuce Cups

Makes: 30     Ready In: 30 mins

Each: 21 cals ~ 1g Total Fat ~ 0.2g Sat Fat ~ 1g Carbs ~ 0g Fibre ~ 2g Protein

## Ingredients

- 145g (1½ cups) bean sprouts/mung beans
- 10 red radish
- bunch fresh coriander (cilantro)
- 1 tbsp grated fresh ginger root
- 1 garlic clove
- ¼ tsp Chinese five spice
- 2 carrots, grated
- 1-2 dashes Tabasco sauce
- 1 lime
- 3 tbsp reduced-salt soy sauce
- 1 tbsp toasted sesame oil
- 2 tsp sesame seeds
- 2 baby gem lettuce heads
- 225g (8oz) Sirloin (New York Strip) steak, all visible fat removed

## Directions

Heat a non-stick sauté pan over a medium heat and add the sesame seeds. Toast until lightly golden, shaking the pan to make sure they don't burn. Once the seeds are toasted, remove from the pan to saucer to prevent further cooking & cool.

Return the pan to a high heat. Remove all traces of visible fat from the steak. Split the garlic clove in half and rub it all over both sides of the steak, then season with the Chinese five spice. Add the steak to the very hot pan and press it down with a spatula. Cook for 3 mins then turn the steak over and cook for a further 3 mins. Remove from the pan to a carving board, cover with foil and rest for 10 mins. Meanwhile, coarsely grate the carrots. Reserve a few coriander/cilantro leaves for decoration, then finely mince the rest. Finely slice the radishes. Juice the lime into a bowl, add the sesame oil, soy sauce, Tabasco sauce and freshly grated ginger. Whisk together to combine. Add the minced coriander, grated carrot and bean sprouts and toss well to combine. Separate out 30 leaves from the lettuce heads. Rinse to clean and spin dry. Divide the dressed salad vegetables between the lettuce leaves. Thinly slice the rested steak and divide this along with the radishes over the salad. Finely scatter over the reserved coriander leaves and sesame seeds. Serve immediately.

# Festive Coronation Turkey Celery Boats

Makes: 30        Ready In: 10 mins

Each: 44 cals ~ 1g Total Fat ~ 0.1g Sat Fat ~ 7g Carbs ~ 1g Fibre ~ 1g Protein

## Ingredients

- 170g (6oz) skinless roasted turkey breast
- 10 celery sticks
- 4 spring onions (scallions)
- 3 tbsp dried cranberries
- 3 tbsp 3% fat soft cheese
- 2 tbsp 0% Greek yogurt
- 1 tbsp Mango chutney
- ½ tsp Madras curry powder
- 4 tsp flaked almonds

## Directions

Heat a non-stick sauté pan over a medium heat and add the flaked almonds. Toast until lightly golden, keeping a close watch and shaking the pan to make sure they don't burn. As soon as the almonds are toasted, remove from the pan to saucer to prevent further cooking and to allow to cool.

Use a vegetable peeler to "de-thread" the celery stalks – this means running the vegetable peeler over the ribbed side of the celery to remove the stringy bits. It takes less than a minute to do this and makes raw celery so much nicer to eat. Cut each stalk into 3 even lengths.

In a small bowl, whisk together the soft cheese, Greek yogurt, mango chutney and curry powder. Shred the cooked turkey into small pieces and roughly chop the cranberries. Add both to the bowl and toss well to combine. Divide the filling between the celery pieces, then sprinkle over the toasted flaked almonds.

Make this nut free? Replace the flaked almonds with 2 tsp of sesame seeds.

Make Ahead Tips: The dressing can be made 24hrs in advance and stored in the fridge. The almonds can also be toasted 2-3 days in advance and stored in an airtight container.

# Delicious Low Fat Dips

## Baba Ganoush (V, Ve)

Serves: 16          Ready In: 45 mins

Per tbsp: 9 cals ~ 1g Total Fat ~ 0.1g Sat Fat ~
1g Carbs ~ 0g Fibre ~ 0g Protein

### Ingredients

- 1 lemon
- 1 small garlic bulb
- 1 red onion
- 2 medium aubergines/eggplant (each about 450g/1lb)
- Small bunch fresh flat-leaf parsley
- ½ tsp rapeseed oil
- ½ tsp freshly ground black pepper
- 2 tbsp tahini paste
- ¼ tsp olive oil
- ½ tsp sea (kosher) salt

### Directions

Preheat the oven to 180C Fan, 400F, Gas Mark 6. Warm a baking sheet.

Use a fork to prick all over the aubergines/eggplants. With a sharp knife, cut the tip off the garlic bulb exposing the tops of the cloves. Place onto a double square of tin foil and drizzle over ¼ tsp olive oil. Seal the garlic clove up the foil. Place both the aubergines/eggplants and garlic parcel onto the baking sheet and roast for 20 mins, then remove, open up the tin foil parcel and allow everything to cool slightly .

Once the whole aubergine/eggplant has roasted, remove it along with the garlic parcel from the baking sheet. Finely dice the red onion and parsley stalks (keep the leaves for later). Heat ½ tsp rapeseed oil in a non-stick sauté pan over a medium heat and sauté the diced onion and parsley stalks for 5 mins until softened. Meanwhile, once the whole aubergines/eggplants have cooled slightly, cut them in half lengthwise, drain off any liquid then scoop out the pulp into a food processor. Squeeze out the roasted garlic paste from the bulb into the mini-food processor (I wear clean rubber kitchen gloves when I do this as it can be messy!). Discard what's left of the garlic bulb once you've extracted the paste. Add the sautéed onions to the mix and squeeze in the juice of the lemon. Add the tahini paste, reserved parsley leaves and a pinch of salt & pepper. Process until smooth, transfer to a serving bowl.

Make Ahead Tip: This can be made 2-3 days in advance and kept in an airtight container in the fridge.

# Caramelised Onion, Apple & Crispy Prosciutto Dip

Serves: 12       Ready In: 45 mins

Per tbsp: 20 cals ~ 1g Total Fat ~ 0.4g Sat Fat ~ 2g Carbs ~ 0g Fibre ~ 1g Protein

## Ingredients

- 1 large yellow onion or 2 medium onions
- 4 slices Prosciutto, all visible fat removed
- 1 firm red eating apple eg Cox, Fuji
- 85g ($^1/_3$ cup) 3% fat soft cheese
- 90g (6 tbsp) half fat crème fraîche
- ½ tsp freshly ground black pepper
- 2 garlic cloves
- 1 tbsp brown sugar
- 1 tbsp rapeseed oil
- 2 tbsp red wine vinegar
- ¼ tsp cayenne pepper
- ¼ tsp sea (kosher) salt

## Directions

Remove any visible fat from the prosciutto and shred. Peel, top and tail the onion. Cut it in quarters from top to bottom and then thinly slice each quarter.

Heat a large non-stick sauté pan over a medium heat. Add the shredded prosciutto and sauté until crispy. Remove from the pan to a saucer and set aside. Return the pan to stove and reduce the heat to medium-low. Add the rapeseed oil and heat for about 30secs then add the onion slices, tossing them well to coat them in the oil. Sauté the onions for 20-25 mins, stirring and tossing occasionally to prevent them sticking, until they are reduced down and golden brown.

Meanwhile, finely mince the garlic cloves. Add the minced garlic to the sauté pan and sauté for 1 min. Turn the heat up to medium and add the vinegar and sugar, toss well to combine and cook for a further 4-5 mins until the liquid has evaporated. Set aside and allow to cool.

In a bowl, whip together the crème fraîche, soft cheese, cayenne, salt and pepper. Peel the apple and coarsely grate this into the bowl. Add in the caramelised onions, scraping in all the juices from the sauté pan. Stir well to combine and transfer to a pretty serving dish. Sprinkle over the reserved crispy prosciutto and serve.

Make Ahead Tip: The crispy prosciutto and caramelised onions can be prepared 2-3 days in advance and kept in an airtight container in the fridge. Assemble the remaining ingredients for the dip shortly before serving.

# Chunky Guacamole (V)

Serves: 12     Ready In: 20 mins + chilling time

Per tbsp: 18 cals ~ 1g Total Fat ~ 0.3g Sat Fat ~ 1g Carbs ~ 0g Fibre ~ 0g Protein

## Ingredients

- 240g (1½ cups) frozen petit pois, defrosted
- 120g (½ cup) 0% Greek yogurt
- 8 spring onions (scallions)
- 2 large, ripe tomatoes
- bunch fresh coriander (cilantro)
- 1 tsp cayenne pepper
- ½ tsp freshly ground black pepper
- 4 large, ripe avocados
- 1 lime
- 2 mild red chilli pepper
- 2 garlic cloves
- 1 tsp ground cumin
- 1 tsp dried oregano
- ½ tsp sea (kosher) salt

## Directions

Put the tomatoes into a heat-proof jug, cover with boiling water and allow to stand for 1 min. Drain the tomatoes and set aside to cool slightly. Remove the pith and seeds from the chilli peppers and finely mince the flesh along with the garlic cloves. Trim the ends from the spring onions/scallions and thinly slice. Remove the leaves from the coriander/cilantro. Set aside 1 tbsp of leaves for decoration and pop into the fridge until required. Finely mince the remaining leaves and stalks. Pop the defrosted petit pois and Greek yogurt into a mini food processor or blender and whiz together until a smooth purée.

Finely grate the zest from the lime into a roomy bowl and then squeeze in the juice. Halve and stone the avocados (saving 1 stone). Use a teaspoon to scoop out the flesh in chunks into the bowl, tossing in the lime juice after adding each ½ avocado to coat in the lime juice. Next add the minced chilli, garlic, onion and coriander/cilantro.

Peel the skin from the tomatoes and finely dice. Add the diced tomato and all the juices to the bowl along with pea/yogurt purée and the remaining seasonings. Use a fork or potato masher to mix everything together really well, roughly mashing the avocado flesh as you mix.

Pop the reserved avocado stone back into the bowl, then cover the dip in kitchen film, not by stretching across the top of the bowl but rather placing into direct contact with the dip mixture. Pop the bowl in the fridge to 1 hr to chill and for the flavours to develop.

To serve, remove the avocado stone and sprinkle over the reserved coriander/cilantro leaves.

# Roasted Mediterranean Vegetable & White Bean Dip (V)

Serves: 20     Ready In: 45 mins

Per tbsp: 12 cals ~ 1g Total Fat ~ 0.1g Sat Fat ~ 1g Carbs ~ 1g Fibre ~ 1g Protein

## Ingredients

- 1 medium aubergine/eggplant (each about 450g/1lb), divided
- 1 medium sized courgette/zucchini
- 120g (1 cup) chestnut (cremini) mushrooms
- 245g (1¼ cups) canned cannellini beans
- 60ml (¼ cup) 0% fat Greek yogurt
- 1 unwaxed organic lemon
- Frylight olive oil spray
- ½ tsp freshly ground black pepper
- 1 red onion
- 2 cloves garlic
- 70g (½ cup) black olives
- 1½ tbsp tahini paste
- Small bunch fresh basil
- ½ tsp ground cumin
- ½ tsp sea (kosher) salt

## Directions

Preheat the oven to 180C Fan, 400F, Gas Mark 6. Warm a baking sheet.

Cut the aubergine/eggplant in half lengthwise, set 1 half to one side. Cut the other half into small dice about the size of your thumbnail. Dice the courgette/zucchini, mushrooms and onion into a similar size too. Finely mince the garlic. Remove the baking sheet from the oven. On one side, place the ½ aubergines/eggplant cut side up and spritz with Frylight then turn it over so that it's cut side down. Spread the diced vegetables over the other side of the baking sheet. Spritz 6 times with Frylight, finely grate over the lemon zest and sprinkle over with the minced garlic and ground cumin. Toss together all diced vegetables. Return the baking sheet to the oven and roast for 20-25 mins, until lightly golden and crispy at the edges. Set aside to cool slightly.

Thoroughly rinse and drain the cannellini beans then transfer to a food processor. Add the tahini paste, Greek yogurt and a pinch of salt and pepper. Squeeze in the juice of the lemon. Scrape out the pulp from the roasted half aubergine/eggplant and add this to the beans. Process the mixture until smooth.

Transfer the cooled, diced roasted vegetables into a bowl. Finely mince the basil leaves and slice the black olives. Stir both of these into the roasted vegetables. Scrape out the bean purée from the processor and fold into the roasted vegetables. Transfer to a serving bowl.

Make Ahead Tip: This can be made 1-2 days in advance and kept in an airtight container in the fridge.

# Roasted Garlic & Pepper Dip (V)

Serves: 12      Ready In: 35 mins

Per tbsp: 14 cals ~ 0g Total Fat ~ 0.0g Sat Fat ~ 2g Carbs ~ 1g Fibre ~ 1g Protein

Ingredients

- 3 red or orange bell peppers
- 1 small garlic bulb
- 240g (1½ cups) cooked chickpeas
- 120g (½ cup) 0% Greek yogurt
- 1 tbsp tomato purée
- 1 tbsp honey
- 1 tbsp lime juice
- 1½ tsp ground cumin
- 1½ tsp ground paprika, plus extra for decoration
- bunch (about a handful) fresh coriander (cilantro)
- ¼ tsp sea (kosher) salt
- ½ tsp freshly ground black pepper

## Directions

Preheat the oven to 180C Fan, 400F, Gas Mark 6.

Use a sharp knife to slice the top off the garlic bulb, then wrap it in a piece of kitchen foil. Cut the red peppers in half. Place the peppers and wrapped garlic bulb onto a roasting dish, pop into the oven and roast for 25 mins. Remove the peppers and garlic from the oven. Set aside the wrapped garlic bulb to cool. Transfer the hot peppers into a heat-proof bowl and cover with cling film. Allow to steam and cool.

Once cooled, peel the skin of the peppers and discard this along with their seeds and stalks. Pop the flesh into a food processor along with the rinsed and drained chickpeas. Squeeze in the softened garlic paste from the roasted bulb (it's a good idea to wear rubber gloves when doing this). Whizz into a purée. Add the spices, yogurt, tomato purée, honey, lime juice, salt and pepper. Pull off 1 tbsp of leaves from the coriander/cilantro stalks and set aside for decoration, then add the rest to the food processor. Pulse together to combine into a textured paste, adding a little more yogurt, only if required to slacken to a "dip" consistency. Transfer to s serving bowl and sprinkle with the reserved herb leaves and a pinch of paprika.

Make Ahead Tip: This can be made 2-3 days in advance and kept in an airtight container in the fridge.

---

# SWEETCORN & BLUE CHEESE DIP (V)

Serves: 14      Ready In: 10 mins

Per tbsp: 16 cals ~ 1g Total Fat ~ 0.5g Sat Fat ~ 1g Carbs ~ 0g Fibre ~ 1g Protein

## Ingredients

- 160g (1 cup) canned no added salt or sugar sweetcorn, drained
- 135ml (½ cup + 1 tbsp) buttermilk
- 150ml (½ cup + 2 tbsp) half fat soured cream
- 40g (¼ cup) lighter feta cheese, crumbled
- 45g (¹/₃ cup) stilton or other blue cheese, crumbled

- 2 sticks celery
- 1 garlic clove
- 2-3 dashes Tabasco sauce
- ¼ tsp black pepper

## Directions

De-thread the celery stalks by running a vegetable peeler over the ribbed side to remove the strings. Finely dice the celery. Make sure that the sweetcorn is thoroughly drained. Crumble the cheeses into a bowl. Finely grate in the garlic clove. Add the buttermilk, sour cream, Tabasco sauce and black pepper. Lightly beat to mix. Add the corn & celery and stir well to combine. Transfer to a serving dish, cover with cling film and chill in the fridge for 30 mins before serving.

Make Ahead Tip: This can be made 1-2 days in advance and kept in the fridge.

# Toasted Pine Nut, Artichoke & Caper Dip (V)

Serves: 12     Ready In: 5 mins

Per tbsp: 24 cals ~ 2g Total Fat ~ 0.3g Sat Fat ~ 1g Carbs ~ 0g Fibre ~ 1g Protein

Ingredients

- 400g (14 oz) tin artichokes, drained and rinsed
- 60g (7 tbsp) pine nuts (pignoli), divided
- 1 garlic clove
- 1 lemon
- 1 tbsp Nonpareille capers (fine baby capers) in brine, drained and rinsed
- 3 tbsp 3% fat soft cheese
- 3 tbsp 0% fat Greek yogurt
- 4 tbsp freshly grated Parmesan cheese
- small bunch (about a handful) fresh flat-leaf parsley

Directions

Drain and rinse the artichokes and capers, then pat dry. Heat a non-stick sauté pan over a medium-low heat and add the pine nuts (pignoli). Toast the nuts, tossing occasionally, for 2-3 mins until lightly golden brown. Alternatively, if you already have the oven on for something else, pop the pine nuts (pignoli) into an oven-proof ramekin and roast them in the oven for about 5-10mins until lightly golden (do check after 5 mins, as the time required will depend on how hot your oven is). Set aside 1 rounded tbsp for later and pour the rest into the bowl of a food processor.

Also set aside 3-4 parsley leaves then add the rest, along with the artichokes and garlic clove to the food processor. Process until finely chopped. Finely grate the zest from the lemon and add this plus ½ its juice to the food processor, along with the capers, soft cheese, Greek yogurt and parmesan. Pulse until well combined. Taste and add a little more lemon juice, if required.

Transfer to a serving bowl. Sprinkle over the reserved toasted pine nuts and decorate with the parsley leaves.

Make Ahead Tip: This can be made 2-3 days in advance and kept in an airtight container in the fridge.

## Cucumber, Mint & Coriander Raita (V)

Serves: 15          Ready In: 15 mins

Per tbsp: 7 cals ~ 0g Total Fat ~ 0.0g Sat Fat ~ 1g Carbs ~ 0g Fibre ~ 1g Protein

Ingredients

- 1 whole English cucumber
- 1-2 green chilli peppers
- large bunch fresh coriander (cilantro)
- ½ tsp sea (kosher) salt
- 480g (4 cups) 0% fat Greek yogurt
- ½ lime
- small bunch fresh mint

Directions

Peel the cucumber and cut in half lengthwise. Scrape out the seeds with a teaspoon and discard. Pat dry the cucumber with kitchen towel. Coarsely grate the cucumber and lay it out on fresh kitchen towel to absorb any excess moisture.

Meanwhile, de-seed the chilli peppers and finely mince. Pick off the mint leaves and discard the stalks. Very finely mince these along with all of the coriander/cilantro (stalks and leaves). Transfer all of these into a bowl along with the yogurt, salt and juice from the ½ lime. Stir well to combine.

Just before serving, tip in the drained, grated cucumber and stir together, then tip into a pretty bowl to serve.

# Black Bean Salsa (V, Ve)

Serves: 12      Ready In: 10 mins

Per tbsp: 10 cals ~ 0g Total Fat ~ 0.0g Sat Fat ~ 1g Carbs ~ 1g Fibre ~ 1g Protein

## Ingredients

- 235g (1 cup + 2½ tbsp) tinned black beans, drained and rinsed
- 14 plum tomatoes
- 2 yellow bell pepper
- 1 red onion
- 1 red chilli pepper
- 1 lime
- 1 tbsp white vinegar
- 1 tbsp extra-virgin olive oil
- 1 tsp ground cumin
- ½-1 tsp Tabasco sauce
- small bunch fresh coriander (cilantro)
- $^1/_8$ tsp sea (kosher) salt
- ¼ tsp ground black pepper

## Directions

Peel and finely dice the red onion. Remove the seeds and pith from the chilli pepper and finely mince along with the coriander/cilantro. Quarter the tomatoes. Remove the seeds and pith from the yellow pepper and dice the flesh.

In a bowl, finely grate the zest of the lime and then squeeze out the juice. Add the olive oil, vinegar, cumin and Tabasco sauce, then whisk well to combine. Add the minced onion, chilli, coriander/cilantro, salt and pepper and whisk again. Finally add the black beans, peppers and tomatoes and toss well to combine. Taste and add more Tabasco if you prefer more spice/heat.

Transfer to a serving bowl.

Make Ahead Tip: This salsa actually benefits from being made in advance as the flavours develop with time. Make 2-3 days in advance and kept in an airtight container in the fridge.

# Herby Pomegranate Salsa (V, Ve)

Serves: 12          Ready In: 10 mins

Per tbsp: 8 cals ~ 0g Total Fat ~ 0.1g Sat Fat ~ 1g Carbs ~ 0g Fibre ~ 0g Protein

## Ingredients

- 1 whole English cucumber
- 14 cherry tomatoes
- 4 spring onions (scallions)
- 110g ($^2/_3$ cup) pomegranate seeds
- small bunch parsley
- small bunch coriander (cilantro)
- small bunch mint
- 1 lemon
- 1 tbsp pomegranate molasses*
- 1 tbsp extra virgin olive oil
- 1 tsp natural caster sugar
- ¼ tsp sea (kosher) salt
- ½ tsp ground black pepper

Note: Pomegranate molasses is widely available in the speciality ingredient section of the supermarket or online. If you don't have it to hand, simply substitute with 2 tsp of honey or maple syrup and 1 tsp of lemon juice.

## Directions

In a bowl, finely grate the zest of the lemon and then squeeze out the juice. Add the olive oil, sugar, pomegranate molasses, salt and pepper, then whisk well to combine. Pick off the leaves from the mint and discard the stalks. Finely mince the mint leaves along with all of the parsley and coriander/cilantro (stalks and leaves). Add to the dressing and toss to combine.

Peel the cucumber and cut in half lengthwise. Scrape out the seeds with a teaspoon and discard. Dice the cucumber flesh. Finely slice the onions. Cut the cherry tomatoes into quarters. Add all these vegetables to the bowl along with the pomegranate seeds.

Toss really well and transfer to a serving bowl.

Make Ahead Tip: This salsa actually benefits from being made in advance as the flavours develop with time. Make 2-3 days in advance and kept in an airtight container in the fridge.

# CRAB, FENNEL & MANGO DIP

Serves: 16       Ready In: 15 mins

Per tbsp: 11 cals ~ 0g Total Fat ~ 0.1g Sat Fat ~ 2g Carbs ~ 0g Fibre ~ 1g Protein

Ingredients

- 240g (8 1/2 oz) white crab meat, fresh, canned or frozen and defrosted
- 2 medium ripe tomatoes
- 1 medium ripe mango
- ½ medium fennel bulb
- 5 spring onions (scallions)
- 2.5cm/1" size piece of fresh root ginger
- 2 limes
- small fresh coriander (cilantro)
- 1 red chilli
- 5-6 stems fresh mint
- 1 garlic clove
- 1 tbsp fish sauce (nam pla)
- 1 stalk lemon grass
- 1 tbsp toasted sesame oil
- 1 tsp soft brown sugar
- 1 tsp sesame seeds
- ½ tsp ground black pepper

Directions

Heat a non-stick sauté pan over a medium heat and add the sesame seeds. Toast until lightly golden, shaking the pan to make sure they don't burn. As soon as they are toasted, remove to a saucer to prevent further cooking and cool.

De-seed the chilli pepper and cut into chunks. Remove the woody end of the lemon grass stalk and any tough outer leaves and roughly chop. Peel the fresh ginger and cut into chunks. Peel the garlic and add this along with the lemon grass, chilli and ginger to the bowl of a mini-food processor. Process until finely chopped. Remove the leaves from the coriander/cilantro and set aside. Add the stalks to the food processor and whizz again to finely mince. Next add the finely grated zest of 1 lime and then squeeze in the juice of both of them. Add the toasted sesame oil, sugar, fish sauce and pepper, then whizz the processor again. Pick over the crab to make sure that there is no shell present then transfer to a bowl and shred with a fork. Peel the mango, cut off the flesh and finely dice it. Add the bowl, scraping in all the mango juices that escaped when dicing the flesh. Dice the tomatoes and add these to the bowl too. Remove the tough core from the fennel, finely dice and add to the bowl. Finely slice the onions and add to the bowl. Pick off the leaves from the mint and discard the stalks. Finely mince the mint and coriander/cilantro leaves and add these to the bowl. Pour over the dressing and toss really well. Transfer to a serving bowl and scatter over the toasted sesame seeds.

Make Ahead Tip: This can be made up to 1 day in advance and kept in the fridge.

# Yogurt, Thyme & Olive Dip (V)

Serves: 8          Ready In: 1 hr 5 mins

Per tbsp: 17 cals ~ 1g Total Fat ~ 0.1g Sat Fat ~ 1g Carbs ~ 0g Fibre ~ 2g Protein

## Ingredients

- 380g (1½ cups) 0% Greek yogurt
- 3 spring onions (scallions), divided
- 4-5 stems fresh thyme
- ½ tsp freshly ground black pepper
- Butter muslin, cheesecloth or kitchen towel
- 15 green olives
- 1 tbsp olive oil, divided
- ¼ tsp cayenne pepper
- ¼ tsp sea (Kosher) salt

## Directions

Line a sieve with muslin or kitchen towel and place it over a bowl. Pour in the yogurt and leave in the fridge to strain for an hour (or overnight), then discard the drained off liquid. Rinse off the brine or oil from the olives and thoroughly pat dry on kitchen towel. Finely slice these along with the onions. Set aside 1 heaped tbsp for garnishing the finished dip. Pull the thyme leaves off the stems and finely mince the leaves. In a bowl, tip in the strained yogurt along with the sliced onions, olives, thyme and salt. In a small ramekin, whisk together the olive oil with the ground peppers. Transfer the yogurt dip into a serving bowl and use a spoon to create a swirl pattern on top. Sprinkle over the reserved onions/olives & drizzle over the spiced oil.

# Ricotta, Watercress & Toasted Walnut Dip (V)

Serves: 10       Ready In: 10 mins

Per tbsp: 22 cals ~ 2g Total Fat ~ 0.8g Sat Fat ~ 1g Carbs ~ 0g Fibre ~ 1g Protein

## Ingredients

- 120g (3½ cups) watercress
- 80g (¹/₃ cup) half fat sour cream
- 1 lemon
- ½ tsp freshly ground black pepper
- 225g (1¾ cups) ricotta cheese
- small bunch fresh flat-leaf parsley
- 15 walnut halves
- ¼ tsp sea (Kosher) salt

## Directions

Chop the walnuts. Heat a sauté pan over a medium heat and add the chopped nuts. Toast until lightly golden, shaking the pan to make sure they don't burn. Once toasted, remove the nuts from the pan to saucer to prevent further cooking, cool. Pick the leaves from the parsley and place into the bowl of a food processor (discard the stems). Remove any really woody stems from the watercress before adding this to the food processor too. Whizz to finely chop. Add the ricotta, sour cream, salt pepper and lemon juice. Process into a purée. Taste, add more lemon juice if required & transfer to a serving bowl. Sprinkle over the toasted walnuts.

# Avocado, Artichoke & Feta Dip (V)

Serves: 20      Ready In: 1 hr 5 mins

Per tbsp: 20 cals ~ 1g Total Fat ~ 0.6g Sat Fat ~ 1g Carbs ~ 0g Fibre ~ 1g Protein

## Ingredients

- 1 red onion
- 2 red chillies
- 1 garlic clove
- 2 lemons
- 240g artichoke hearts
- 20 pimento stuffed green olives
- 1 ripe avocado
- 190g lighter feta cheese
- 150g ricotta cheese
- bunch coriander (cilantro)
- 1 tsp rapeseed oil

## Directions

De-seed the chillies and finely mince along with the peeled garlic clove. Remove the leaves from the coriander/cilantro and set aside for later. Finely mince the stalks. Peel and finely dice the red onion. Heat the rapeseed oil in a non-stick sauté pan over a medium heat. Add the onion and sauté for 8 mins until lightly golden and softened. Add the minced chillies, garlic and herb stalks and cook for a further 2 mins, then remove from the heat and transfer to a plate to cool.

Put the coriander/cilantro leaves into the bowl of a food processor and chop very finely. Add the cooled sautéed vegetables and whizz again. Scoop out the avocado flesh and add this to the processor along with the juice from the lemons and ricotta cheese. Process into a smooth purée.

Thoroughly rinse the artichokes and olives, drain and tip onto kitchen towel and pat dry. Dice the artichokes and transfer to a bowl. Add the avocado purée mixture and stir well to combine. Crumble in the feta cheese and stir this through the dip.

Transfer the dip into a pretty serving dish. Slice the pimento-stuffed olives and scatter over the dip before serving.

# Green Goddess Dip (V)

Serves: 8     Ready In: 1 hr 5 mins

Per tbsp: 9 cals ~ 0g Total Fat ~ 0.0g Sat Fat ~ 1g Carbs ~ 0g Fibre ~ 1g Protein

## Ingredients

- 150ml (½ cup + 2 tbsp) buttermilk
- 60g (¼ cup) lightest mayonnaise
- 10 spring onions (scallions)
- 1 lemon
- 2 tbsp Nonpareille capers (fine baby capers) in brine, drained and rinsed
- 3 garlic cloves
- bunch fresh basil leaves
- ¼ tsp sea (Kosher) salt
- ½ tsp freshly ground black pepper

## Directions

Rinse off the brine from the capers and thoroughly pat dry on kitchen towel. Roughly chop the capers and finely slice the onions. Set aside 1 heaped tbsp for garnishing the finished dip, and put the remainder into a bowl.

Place the garlic into the bowl of a pestle and mortar along with the salt. Grind together really thoroughly to form a paste. If you don't have a pestle and mortar, pop the garlic and salt onto a chopping board and simply use the flat side of a kitchen knife to work together into a paste.

Set aside a sprig of tiny basil leaves for decoration then strip the remaining leaves from the basil stems and then transfer to a food processor. Whizz to finely chop. Add the mayonnaise, buttermilk, garlic paste, pepper and juice from ½ lemon. Pulse to combine but don't overwork the mixture. Pour the mixture into the bowl with the onions and capers and stir well to combine. Taste and add more lemon juice if required.

Transfer the dip into a serving bowl and sprinkle over the reserved onions/capers and decorate with the sprig of basil leaves.

Make Ahead Tip: Transfer to an airtight container and keep for 1-2 days in advance in the fridge.

# Hot Artichoke, Spinach & Cheese Dip (V)

Serves: 16      Ready In: 20 mins

Per tbsp: 11 cals ~ 1g Total Fat ~ 0.3g Sat Fat ~ 1g Carbs ~ 0g Fibre ~ 1g Protein

## Ingredients

- 240g (1½ cups) tinned artichokes
- 6 spring onions (scallions)
- 3 garlic cloves
- 155g (1 cup) frozen spinach leaves, defrosted & drained
- 175g (¾ cup) 3% fat soft cheese
- 60g (¼ cup) half fat crème fraîche
- 25g (¼ cup) finely grated parmesan cheese
- 1 red chilli pepper
- ½ lemon
- ½ tsp sea salt
- ½ tsp freshly ground black pepper
- 2-3 dashes Tabasco sauce

## Directions

Preheat the oven to 180C Fan, 400F, Gas Mark 6.

Rinse the artichoke hearts, cut in half and drain on kitchen towel. Set aside 1 tbsp parmesan cheese. In a bowl, whisk together the remaining parmesan, soft cheese, crème fraîche, Tabasco, salt and pepper. Deseed the chilli pepper and finely mince. Add this to the bowl and grate in the garlic cloves. Thinly slice the onions and add to the bowl. Squeeze in the juice of the lemon and mix together to combine.

Squeeze out as much water as possible from the spinach then add this to the bowl too. Chop up the drained artichoke hearts and add to the bowl. Use a fork to combine together, breaking up the spinach and making sure everything is well combined. Transfer to a lightly greased baking dish and sprinkle over the reserved parmesan cheese. Pop into the oven and bake for 15-18mins until hot and golden.

Make Ahead Tip: This can be prepared up to 24 hrs in advance then bake as above but for 18-20 mins, before serving.

# Hot Chunky BBQ Dip

Serves: 15    Ready In: 25 mins

Per tbsp: 8 cals ~ 0g Total Fat ~ 0.0g Sat Fat ~ 1g Carbs ~ 0g Fibre ~ 0g Protein

## Ingredients

- 6 medium vine tomatoes
- 1 tbsp dark brown sugar
- 1 red chilli pepper
- ½ tsp ground cumin
- ½ tsp dry mustard
- ½ tsp dried oregano
- 1 tbsp tomato purée
- 1 tsp rapeseed (canola) oil
- ½ tsp ground black pepper

- 2 red onions
- 2 garlic cloves
- ½ tsp smoked paprika
- ½ tsp chipotle chilli powder
- ¹/₈ tsp ground allspice
- 1 tbsp fresh ginger, grated
- 1½ tbsp balsamic vinegar
- ½ lime
- ¼ tsp sea (kosher) salt

## Directions

Place the tomatoes in a large heat-proof bowl and cover with boiling water. Leave for 1½ mins then drain away the water, refresh with cold water, drain again and allow the tomatoes.

Meanwhile, de-seed the red chilli pepper and finely mince along with the garlic cloves. Peel then finely grate the ginger root. Peel the onions and roughly dice.

Heat the rapeseed oil in a non-stick sauté or frying pan over a medium heat. Add the onion and cook for 5 mins until softened, stirring occasionally. While the onion cooks, slip the skins off the tomatoes and roughly chop.

Once the onions are softened and lightly golden, add the minced garlic, chilli and ginger and cook for a further 1 minute. Next add all the spices and dried oregano then cook 30 secs. Finally stir in the chopped tomatoes, tomato purée, balsamic vinegar, sugar, salt and pepper. Stir well to combine and bring up to a gentle simmer. Cook for 15 mins or until slightly thickened, stirring occasionally.

When ready to serve, squeeze over the juice of the ½ lime and transfer to a warm serving dish.

Make Ahead Tip: This can be prepared up to 2-3 days in advance, reheat in a saucepan on the stove and add the lime juice just before serving.

# Hot & Spicy Roasted Corn & Pepper Dip (V)

Serves: 20    Ready In: 20 mins

Per tbsp: 16 cals ~ 1g Total Fat ~ 0.4g Sat Fat ~ 1g Carbs ~ 0g Fibre ~ 1g Protein

## Ingredients

- 2 whole corn on the cob (ears of corn)
- 8 cherry tomatoes
- 1 red chilli pepper
- ½ jar pickled jalapeno peppers
- 75g (²/₃ cup) grated half-fat cheddar cheese
- 150g (²/₃ cup) 3% fat soft cheese
- 100g (½ cup less 1 tbsp) half-fat sour cream
- Frylight olive oil spray
- ½ tsp freshly ground black pepper

- 2 red bell peppers
- 1 red onion
- 2 cloves garlic
- ½ lime
- 1 tsp dried oregano
- ½ tsp ground cumin
- 2-3 dashes Tabasco sauce
- 1 tsp rapeseed oil

## Directions

Clean the corn cobs, removing any husk and stringy bits. Heat a griddle pan over a medium high heat. Spritz the corn with Frylight and place onto the griddle to toast the corn. Cook the corn for 8-10 mins, turning them over several times so that the cobs are golden toasted all over. Remove from the grill and set aside to cool slightly. Meanwhile, thoroughly rinse the pickled jalapeno peppers to remove as much of the salt as possible, then drain and roughly chop.

Preheat the oven to 180C Fan, 400F, Gas Mark 6.

Deseed the chilli pepper and finely mince along with the garlic cloves. Dice the onion and bell peppers. Heat the rapeseed oil in a non-stick sauté pan over a medium heat and add the onions. Sauté for 3-4 mins and then add the diced bell peppers, continue to sauté until softened and golden, around another 5 mins. Add the minced chilli and garlic, cook for a further 1 min, then add the cumin and oregano, toss well to combine and remove from the heat.

Meanwhile, whisk together the soft cheese, crème fraîche, Tabasco and pepper. Finely grate in the zest from the lime and squeeze in the juice. Use a sharp knife to remove the corn kernels from the cobs, holding the cobs upright and slicing down the side of the cobs. Cut the cherry tomatoes into quarter and add these along with all the corn kernels. Add the chopped, rinsed pickles & the sautéed veg. Give everything a thorough mix. Set aside 2 tbsp grated cheese, add the remainder to the bowl & mix. Transfer to a lightly greased baking dish & sprinkle over the reserved cheese. Pop into the oven & bake for 15-18mins until hot and golden. Make Ahead Tip: Prepare up to 24 hrs in advance then bake for 18-20 mins.

# Healthier Dippers, Dunkers & Chips

## Mustard & Cumin Seeded Parsnip Fingers (V, Ve)

Serves: 12      Ready In: 45 mins

Per Serving of 3: 43 cals ~ 2g Total Fat ~ 0.2g Sat Fat ~ 5g Carbs ~ 2g Fibre ~ 1g Protein

### Ingredients

- 6 medium parsnips
- 1 tbsp rapeseed oil
- 1 tsp cumin seeds
- 1 tsp mustard seeds
- ½ tsp black peppercorns
- ½ tsp sea (Kosher) salt, divided

### Directions

Preheat the oven to 180C Fan, 400F, Gas Mark 6. Add the oil to the roasting tin and put it in the oven to heat up.

Peel the parsnips then cut in half lengthwise, then cut each of these, lengthwise, into 3 fingers. Bring a pan of water to the boil, add ¼ tsp salt and the parsnips. Cook for 3 mins then quickly drain.

Meanwhile, in a pestle and mortar, coarsely grind the black peppercorns. Next add the cumin seeds and grind again. Lastly, add the mustard for one final grinding then add ¼ tsp sea salt and mix together. Grind the seeds in this order which takes into account that the mustard seeds are much softer than the cumin seeds and that the peppercorns are the hardest of all. If you don't have a pestle and mortar, use the end of a rolling pin to crush the seeds in a small ramekin.

Remove the hot roasting tin from the oven and tip the tin to spread out the oil. Add the drained parsnips and lightly toss to coat. Sprinkle over the crushed spices and return to the oven. Roast for 25-30mins until crispy and golden. Serve hot.

# Blooming Onion (V, Ve)

Serves: 8      Ready In: 45 mins + soaking time

Per Serving: 45 cals ~ 2g Total Fat ~ 0.1g Sat Fat ~ 6g Carbs ~ 1g Fibre ~ 1g Protein

Ingredients

- 1 very large yellow onion (about 340g/12oz)
- 2 garlic cloves
- 35g wholemeal bread (1 slice)
- 2 tsp dried oregano
- 1 tsp Chinese five spice
- 1 tsp mixed spice
- ½ tsp ground cumin
- ½ tsp cayenne pepper
- 1 tsp freshly ground black pepper
- Frylight olive oil spray
- 2 tsp rapeseed oil

## Directions

You will need 2 very sharp knives for this dish, a large knife and a smaller vegetable paring knife. Fill a large bowl $^2/_3$rds full with cold water and ice cubes.

Slice the top off the onion and carefully peel off the skin, making sure that you keep the onion root in tact. Use the large knife to cut down $^2/_3$rds of the way from top to bottom across the centre of onion. Turn the onion half way round and repeat. So now you have an onion which you have partially cut into quarter segments but the root is still in tact as you've only cut down $^2/_3$rds of the way through the onion. Repeat this process to cut each quarter in half again and then half again. Now turn the onion over so that the root is uppermost and use your sharp small knife to slice down each existing cut taking it closer to the root but avoiding cutting too close to the root. Turn the onion back over and place it in the bowl of iced water and leave for 25 mins (or in the fridge overnight).

Preheat the oven to 180C Fan, 400F, Gas Mark 6.

Remove the onion from the iced water and place root side up on some kitchen towel to drain.

Peel the garlic cloves and pop them into a mini-food processor. Whizz to finely chop. Add the bread slice in chunks and whizz again process into breadcrumbs. Add all the seasonings and pulse to combine. Finally, add the rapeseed oil and pulse again to ensure that all the crumbs are coated in oil.

Turn the onion back over. The onion should have spread-out ("flowered") in the iced water, but give it a quick check-over and separate any layers that haven't separated. Place 1 tbsp of breadcrumbs in the centre of the roasting dish and sit the onion, root side down, on top of them. Spritz the onion 6 times with Frylight, then sprinkle over the breadcrumbs, taking care to make sure that they fall in between all the layers. I do this by sprinkling the crumbs in a teaspoon and work 1 segment at a time. Once you have divided the breadcrumbs evenly over the onion, spray again with Frylight and pop it into the oven. Roast for 25-30 mins until the crumbs are golden brown and the onion is tender. Remove from the oven and serve.

Make Ahead Tip: The onion can be cut and left to soak in the iced water in the fridge up to 24 hrs in advance. The breadcrumbs can also be prepared 24hrs in advance and kept in an airtight container in the fridge. Drain & dry the onion as described above and then follow the directions to assemble and roast it.

# CHEESY COURGETTE CRISPS (V)

Serves: 14     Ready In: 45 mins

Per Serving: 84 cals ~ 4g Total Fat ~ 1.5g Sat Fat ~ 5g Carbs ~ 2g Fibre ~ 1g Protein

## Ingredients

- 2 medium courgette/zucchini, cut into ½ cm/¼" slices (about 400g/3½ cups)
- 130g wholemeal baguette, processed into breadcrumbs (about 1¼ cups)
- 100g (3½ oz) half-fat mature cheddar cheese
- 75g (½ cup) plain (all-purpose) flour
- 2 UK medium (US large) free range eggs
- 2 tsp dried herbs de Provence
- 1 tsp freshly ground black pepper
- 1 tbsp rapeseed oil

## Directions

Preheat the oven to 180C Fan, 400F, Gas Mark 6. Warm 2 baking sheets.

Put the bread into a food processor and pulse into breadcrumbs. Spread out onto the baking sheets and toast in the oven for 3-5 mins until golden and crispy. Remove from the oven, place into a shallow bowl and allow to cool completely. Wipe off the baking sheets and return them to the oven to keep hot.

Slice the courgette/zucchini into ½ cm/¼" discs. Cut the cheese into rough dice and grind into fine crumbs in the food processor. Add these to the cooled, toasted breadcrumbs along with the dried herbs and black pepper. Toss well to combine.

Break the eggs into a shallow dish, add 1 tbsp cold water and lightly whisk together. Place the flour in a third shallow dish.

Set the bowls out in row, left to right, starting with the flour, followed by the eggs and finishing with the cheesy breadcrumbs. Now, working in batches, toss the courgette/zucchini discs in the flour, shake off the excess, then dip them into the egg mix, followed by crumbs. Lay the completed discs in a single layer onto a tray until all the discs have been coated.

Take the hot baking sheets out of the oven and coat each one in ½ tbsp of rapeseed oil, using a spatula to spread the oil out so that it coats the entire sheet. Add the coated vegetable slices, laying them out so that they don't overlap. Return the baking sheets to the oven and cook for 12 mins, then take them out of the oven and turn them over. Return to the oven and cook for a further 5-10 mins until crispy and golden. Serve hot.

# Smoky Rosemary Sweet Potato Wedges (V, Ve)

Serves: 8          Ready In: 45 mins

Per Serving of 3: 66 cals ~ 2g Total Fat ~ 0.2g Sat Fat ~ 11g Carbs ~ 1g Fibre ~ 1g Protein

## Ingredients

- 1 tbsp finely minced fresh rosemary leaves
- 1 tsp smoked paprika
- 1 tbsp rapeseed oil
- 3 medium sweet potatoes
- ¼ tsp sea (kosher) salt

## Directions

Preheat the oven to 180C Fan, 400F, Gas Mark 6. Warm a roasting tin in the oven.

Scrub clean the sweet potatoes (no need to peel) and pat dry. Cut into quarters lengthwise and then cut each quarter in half lengthwise to create 8 wedges per potato. Finely mince the rosemary leaves and transfer to a bowl. Add the paprika, salt and rapeseed oil and mix. Add the potato wedges and toss until they are all covered in the spicy oil.

Remove the hot roasting tin from the oven. Tip in the wedges, spread them out and return it to the oven. Roast for 25-30mins until crispy and golden. Serve hot.

# Spiced Tortilla Dunkers (V, Ve)

Serves: 16          Ready In: 20 mins

Per Serving of 3: 39 cals ~ 0g Total Fat ~ 0.1g Sat Fat ~ 7g Carbs ~ 2g Fibre ~ 1g Protein

## Ingredients

- ½ tsp ground coriander
- ¼ tsp smoked paprika
- ¼ tsp fresh ground black pepper
- 6x 20 cm (8") tortilla wraps
- 1 tsp ground cumin
- $^1/_8$ tsp ground ginger
- $^1/_8$ tsp sea (kosher) salt
- Frylight olive oil spray

## Directions

Preheat the oven to 180C Fan, 400F, Gas Mark 6. Put a baking sheet into warm.

In a small bowl, mix together the cumin, coriander, paprika, ginger, salt and pepper. Cut the tortillas into $^1/_8$ wedges (so cut into quarters and then cut each quarter in half). Remove the baking sheet from the oven and lay out the tortilla triangles in a single layer. From a height, spritz evenly with 6 sprays of Frylight spray and sprinkle over half the spice mix. Turn the triangles over and repeat.

Pop the baking sheet back into the hot oven. After 10 mins, remove from the oven and turn the chips over, then return to the oven for another 5 mins, until golden and crispy. Transfer to a wire rack to cool or serve warm.

Make Ahead Tip: Keep for 3-4 days in an airtight container.

# Roasted Asparagus & Parma Ham Dippers

Serves: 12     Ready In: 20 mins

Per Serving of 3: 40 cals ~ 2g Total Fat ~ 0.3g Sat Fat ~ 1g Carbs ~ 1g Fibre ~ 5g Protein

## Ingredients

- 36 fresh, medium asparagus spears
- 12 slices Parma ham
- ½ tsp rapeseed (canola) oil
- freshly ground black pepper

## Directions

Preheat the oven to 180C fan, 350F, Gas Mark 6. Put a baking sheet into warm.

Trim the woody ends off the asparagus spears. Remove all visible fat from the Parma ham slices and cut into thirds lengthwise and then wrap each asparagus spear with a strip of ham. Remove the baking sheet from the oven and add the rapeseed oil. Use a spatula to spread it out over the sheet. Place the wrapped asparagus spears onto the greased baking sheet and season with freshly ground black pepper and place back into the oven to roast. After 8 mins, remove from the oven and turn them over then return to the oven for a further 5-7 mins until lightly golden and tender.

Make Ahead Tip: The asparagus fingers can be fully prepared up to 24 hrs in advance and kept in an airtight container in the fridge, then roast as directed above.

# Salt & Cider Vinegar Vegetable Chips (V, Ve)

Serves: 8     Ready In: 35 mins

Per Serving: 69 cals ~ 1g Total Fat ~ 0.2g Sat Fat ~ 12g Carbs ~ 2g Fibre ~ 1g Protein

## Ingredients

- 2 whole uncooked beetroot
- 2 medium parsnips
- 1 tbsp cider vinegar
- ½ tsp freshly ground black pepper
- V-slicer or mandoline or slicing disc in a food processor (all optional)
- 2 medium sweet potato
- 1½ tsp rapeseed oil
- ¼ tsp sea (Kosher) salt

## Directions

Preheat the oven to 180C Fan, 400F, Gas Mark 6. Warm 2 non-stick baking sheets.

Scrub the vegetables clean (no need to peel). Top and tail the beetroot and parsnip (you may want to wear rubber gloves as you do this). Pat the roots dry.

Using a V-slicer or mandoline or a food processor fitted with a slicing disc, finely slice vegetables. Alternatively, use a very sharp knife to very thinly slice the vegetables. Pat the vegetable slices dry with kitchen towel.

In a large bowl, whisk together the oil, vinegar, ground pepper and salt. Add the parsnips and sweet potatoes and toss. Remove from the bowl, then add the beetroot slices and toss these too (keeping the beetroot slices separate stops them from staining the other vegetable slices pink)!

Remove the baking sheets Lay the vegetable slices out onto the baking sheets in a single layer, making sure that they don't overlap (you may need to cook in more than 1 batch if necessary). Put into the oven and bake for 8 mins, then take out the oven and turn all the slices over. Return to the oven and bake for a further 5 mins, check whether the slices are crispy. Different sized slices will cook at different rates so transfer cooked ones to a wire rack to cool and return those that need more cooking to the oven for another 5mins, check again and continue until all the chips are cooked crisply, then transfer to the wire rack when cooked.

Make Ahead Tip: Transfer the crisps to an airtight container to keep for 2-3 days.

## Smoked Mackerel Pâté

Serves: 10          Ready In: 15 mins + 2 hrs chilling

Per tbsp: 30 cals ~ 2g Total Fat ~ 0.6g Sat Fat ~ 1g Carbs ~ 0g Fibre ~ 2g Protein

### Ingredients

- 225g (8½ oz) skinned smoked mackerel fillet
- 230g (1 cup) 3% fat soft cream cheese
- 6 cornichons (cocktail baby gherkins)
- 1 tsp Nonpareille capers
- ¼ lemon, squeezed
- ½ tsp ground black pepper

### Directions

Remove the skin & any bones from the mackerel fillet. To remove excess salt, rinse, drain and pat dry with kitchen towel the mackerel, capers and gherkins. Roughly chop the gherkins and capers, and then place into a mini food processor and blend. Break the mackerel fillet onto 3 or 4 pieces and add to the processor along with the soft cheese, lemon juice and freshly ground black pepper. Blend until smooth.

If you don't have a food processor, simply chop the gherkins and capers as finely as you can. Mash the mackerel fillets with a fork and then combine all the ingredients together. The pate will be a little more rustic in texture but will still taste delicious. Transfer to a ramekin. The pâté can be served immediately but it will be firmer if allowed to chill for 2 hrs before serving.

Make Ahead Tip: You can store the pâté in its dish and covered in kitchen film in the fridge for up to 1-2 days.

# Spiced Red Lentil & Sweet Potato Pâté (V, Ve)

Serves: 10      Ready In: 25 mins + 2 hrs chilling

Per tbsp: 15 cals ~ 1g Total Fat ~ 0.3g Sat Fat ~ 0g Carbs ~ 0g Fibre ~ 2g Protein

## Ingredients

- 1 medium sweet potato
- ½ red onion
- 1 garlic clove
- 5 stems fresh coriander (cilantro)
- 420ml (1¾ cups) reduced salt vegetable stock
- ½ tsp freshly ground black pepper
- ½ lime

- 135g red lentils
- 1 red chilli pepper
- ½ tsp ground cumin
- ½ tsp cayenne pepper
- 1 tsp rapeseed (canola) oil
- ¼ tsp sea (kosher) salt

## Directions

De-seed the red chilli and remove any white membrane inside the chilli. Remove the leaves from the fresh coriander/cilantro and set aside. Finely mince the stems along with chilli and the peeled garlic clove. Peel the red onion and finely dice. Peel the sweet potato and cut into chunks.

Heat the rapeseed oil in a non-stick sauté pan over a medium-low heat and add the onion. Cook for 5-8 mins until softened, add the minced garlic, chilli and coriander stems and cook for a further min. Add the ground cumin, sweet potato chunks and red lentils and toss well. Pour in the hot vegetable stock and bring up to a gentle simmer. Cover with a pan lid and cook for 15-20 mins until the lentils and potato are completely tender. Drain away any excess liquid remaining in the pan then cover with the pan lid and allow to sit to one side for 5 mins.

Add the salt, pepper and juice from the ½ lime then mash together into a course purée. Allow to cool completely then roughly chop the retained coriander/cilantro leaves and stir these into the pâté. Transfer to a pretty serving dish, cover with kitchen film and chill in the fridge for 1 hr. Return to room temperature for 30 mins and dust with cayenne pepper before serving.

Make Ahead Tip: You can store the pâté in its dish and covered in kitchen film in the fridge for up to 1-2 days.

# CHICKEN LIVER PARFAITS

Serves: 10      Ready In: 25 mins + 2 hrs chilling

Per tbsp: 18 cals ~ 1g Total Fat ~ 0.3g Sat Fat ~ 0g Carbs ~ 0g Fibre ~ 2g Protein

Ingredients

- 370g (13 oz) organic free-range chicken livers
- 3 garlic cloves
- 2 shallots
- 1 tsp rapeseed (canola) oil, divided
- 1 tbsp Cognac
- 1 tsp fresh thyme
- 1 tbsp Dijon mustard
- 4 tbsp half fat crème fraîche
- ½ tsp ground mace
- ¼ tsp allspice
- ¼ tsp freshly ground black pepper
- ¼ tsp sea (kosher) salt

Note: This pâté can also be made with duck livers if you are able to source them.

Directions

Rinse and drain the livers. Pat dry and trim away any sinew. Finely mince the shallot, garlic and thyme leaves.

Heat ½ tsp of rapeseed oil in a non-stick sauté pan over a medium-low heat and add the shallot. Cook for 5-8 mins until softened, add the garlic and cook for a further min. Remove from the pan and set aside. Return the pan to stove top, add a further ½ tsp of rapeseed oil and increase the heat to medium. Add the livers to the hot pan and cook for 5 mins, turning once. Add the Cognac to the pan and allow it to bubble down then remove the pan from the heat. Transfer the cooked livers and all their juices into a food processor. Add the sautéed shallots and garlic along with thyme, mustard, crème fraîche, mace and allspice.

Process the mixture in the food processor until it is completely smooth. Transfer to a pretty serving dish, cover with kitchen film and chill in the fridge for 2 hrs. Return to room temperature for 30 mins before serving.

Make Ahead Tip: You can store the pâté in its dish and covered in kitchen film in the fridge for up to 1-2 days.

# Broad Bean & Basil Spread (V)

Serves: 12        Ready In: 30 mins + 2 hrs chilling

Per tbsp: 29 cals ~ 2g Total Fat ~ 0.4g Sat Fat ~ 1g Carbs ~ 1g Fibre ~ 1g Protein

## Ingredients

- 225g (1½ cups) frozen de-skinned broad beans (fava beans), defrosted
- 45g ($^1/_3$ cup) pine nuts (pignoli)
- 1 ripe avocado
- 3 garlic cloves
- 25g (4 tbsp) finely grated parmesan cheese
- good bunch fresh basil
- 1 unwaxed organic lemon
- ¼ tsp freshly ground black pepper

## Directions

Heat a non-stick sauté pan over a medium-low heat and add the pine nuts (pignoli). Toast the nuts, tossing occasionally, for 2-3 mins until lightly golden brown. Alternatively, if you already have the oven on for something else, pop the pine nuts (pignoli) into an oven-proof ramekin and roast them in the oven for 5-10mins until lightly golden (do check after 5 mins, as the time required will depend on how hot your oven is). Remove to a saucer and allow to cool.

Place the peeled garlic cloves into a mini-food processor and whizz until finely chopped. Add the defrosted and drained broad beans (fava beans) to the processor and whiz again to roughly chop. Finely grate the zest from half of the lemon. Add this to the processor along with the cooled pine nuts (pignoli) and parmesan cheese. Pulse again. Strip the leaves from the basil stems and scoop out the flesh from the avocado. Add this to the processor along with the juice from ½ lemon and the black pepper. Pulse again into a chunky paste. Taste to check the seasoning and add more lemon juice if required.

Make Ahead Tip: You can make this up to the stage before adding the basil and avocado and store in the fridge for 24 hrs. Only add the avocado, basil and lemon just before serving to keep this spread zesty and fresh.

# Roasted Mushroom & Garlic Terrine (V, Ve)

Serves: 10     Ready In: 30 mins + 2 hrs chilling

Per tbsp: 17 cals ~ 1g Total Fat ~ 0.1g Sat Fat ~ 1g Carbs ~ 0g Fibre ~ 1g Protein

## Ingredients

- 3 tbsp balsamic vinegar, divided
- Frylight olive oil spray
- Juice from ½ lemon
- bunch fresh parsley
- 15 walnut halves
- $^1/_8$ tsp sea (kosher) salt
- ¼ tsp ground black pepper
- 1 red onion
- 3 garlic cloves, unpeeled
- 65g ($^1/_3$ cup) dried green lentils
- 150ml (½ cup + 2 tbsp) vegetable stock
- 175g (1½ cups) chestnut (baby bella) mushrooms
- ½ medium aubergine (eggplant), cut in half lengthwise c.135g/5 oz

## Directions

Preheat the oven to 180C Fan, 400F, Gas Mark 6. Put a roasting tin into warm

Place the rinsed and drained lentils into a saucepan and cover with the vegetable stock. Bring up to a simmer and cook for 20-25 mins until tender.

Peel, top and tail the shallot and cut into quarters and clean the mushrooms. Put these in a bowl and sprinkle over 1½ tbsp balsamic vinegar. Toss to coat. Remove the roasting tin from the oven and tip in the mushrooms and shallot. Add the aubergine/eggplant cut side up and the unpeeled garlic cloves. Spritz with 3 sprays of Frylight. Turn the aubergine/eggplant over so that it is cut side down. Return the tin to the oven. After 20 mins, add the walnuts to the tin, stir and return to the oven for a further 5 mins.

Remove the roasted vegetables from the oven, tip onto a plate and allow to cool enough to handle. Drain the cooked lentils. Once cool enough to handle, peel the garlic cloves. Scrap the cooked inner flesh from the skin of the aubergine/eggplant and put this into a mini food processor (discard the skin) along with all the roasted vegetables and nuts. Squeeze in the juice of the ½ lemon, the remaining 1½ tbsp balsamic vinegar, salt, pepper and roughly chopped parsley. Process the ingredients into a rough pâté then transfer to a round terrine dish, pushing down firmly with the back of a spoon. Cover with kitchen film and chill for 1-2 hrs.

Make Ahead Tip: You can store the terrine in its dish and covered in kitchen film in the fridge for up to 3-4 days.

## Aromatic Sesame Bagel Crispy Bakes (V, Ve)

Serves: 12          Ready In: 8 mins + chilling time

Per slice: 34 cals ~ 1g Total Fat ~ 0.1g Sat Fat ~ 6g Carbs ~ 0g Fibre ~ 1g Protein

Ingredients

- 1 tsp Chinese five spice
- 1 tbsp reduced salt soy sauce
- ¼ tsp ground ginger
- ¼ tsp fresh ground black pepper
- 2 tsp toasted sesame oil
- 1 tsp sesame seeds
- 6x mini plain bagels

Directions

Chill the bagels in the fridge for 1 hr before slicing.

Preheat the oven to 180C Fan, 400F, Gas Mark 6. Put a baking sheet into the oven to warm.

In a small bowl, whisk together the spices, soy sauce and oil. Slice each mini bagel into 4 thin slices. Remove the baking sheet from the oven and spread out the bagel slices on it. Brush the slices with half of the spicy mixture. Turn them over and brush over the remainder of the mix. From a good height, sprinkle over sesame seeds. Turn the triangles over and repeat.

Pop the baking sheet into the hot oven. After 10 mins, remove from the oven and turn the chips over, then return to the oven for another 5 mins, until golden and crispy. Transfer to a wire rack to cool or serve warm.

Store & Keep Tip: Transfer the cooled triangles to an airtight container to keep for 3-4 days.

# Melba Toast (V, Ve)

Serves: 12        Ready In: 8 mins

Per 2 triangles: 38 cals ~ 1g Total Fat ~ 0.1g Sat Fat ~ 6g Carbs ~ 1g Fibre ~ 5g Protein

## Ingredients

* 6 slices soya & linseed bread slices eg Vogels

## Directions

Heat a grill or broiler to a medium heat. Toast the bread slices on both sides until lightly browned. Remove from the grill/broiler and slice off the crusts. Next, carefully split the toasts in two horizontally through the centre to make 2 thin squares, then cut each square in half diagonally to create 2 triangles. A serrated knife is useful to do this. Lay the triangles back onto the grill pan, untoasted side uppermost and return to the grill/broiler. Watch them like a hawk to make sure they don't burn. The Melba Toast is done when lightly toasted, golden brown and crisp. You may find that some triangles toast more quickly than others, so keep checking and remove the triangles as they are done, continuing to toast until all are done.

# Garlic Bruschetta (V, Ve)

Makes: 30      Ready In: 35 mins

Each: 32 cals ~ 1g Total Fat ~ 0.1g Sat Fat ~ 6g Carbs ~ 0g Fibre ~ 1g Protein

## Ingredients

- 300g (10½ oz) French baguette bread
- 1 tbsp rapeseed oil, divided
- ½ tsp freshly ground black pepper
- 1 bulb garlic
- 1 tbsp white wine vinegar
- ¼ tsp sea (kosher) salt

## Directions

Preheat the oven to 180C Fan, 400F, Gas Mark 6.

Use a sharp knife to slice the top off the garlic bulb, then wrap it in a piece of kitchen foil. Place onto a roasting dish, pop into the oven and roast for 25 mins. Remove from the oven and set aside to cool.

Once cool enough to handle, unwrap the garlic bulb and squeeze out all of the cooked garlic paste into a bowl (it can be helpful to wear rubber gloves to do this)! Add ½ tsp rapeseed oil, vinegar salt and pepper whisk together.

Place a baking sheet into the oven to warm. Slice the French stick into 30 thin slices and spread with the garlic spread. Remove the baking sheet from the oven and oil with ½ tbsp of rapeseed oil. Lay out the bread slices evenly across the baking sheets, lightly pressing them into the oiled surface. Place in the oven and bake for 10-15 mins until golden brown and crispy.

Make Ahead Tip: These can be made 2-3 days in advance, store in an airtight tin. To serve them warm, pop onto a baking sheet & heat in a warm oven for 4-5mins.

# A Note from the Author - Your Feedback

Thank you for choosing my Low Fat Dips, Skinny Nibbles & Healthier Dippers 50+ Recipe Cookbook. *Your feedback is very important to me* and I would love to know what you think of the recipes in this cookbook, are any particular favourites? I would greatly appreciate your feedback with an honest review on the website that you purchased your book.

*Firstly, I want to understand* which dishes you have enjoyed the most, so I can develop more recipes that will be popular with my readers.

*Secondly as an independent author,* competing with the large publishers and their huge marketing budgets is, well, challenging. *Reviews go such a long way towards levelling the playing field.* If you could spare a few minutes to write an honest review, it would be *so helpful and very much appreciated.* Many, many thanks!

# Further Low Fat Cookbooks

You may also be interested in further books from Milly White.

## Easy Low Fat & Low Cholesterol Mediterranean Diet Recipe Cookbook

Studies have repeatedly linked the Mediterranean Diet with numerous health benefits including lower cholesterol, a healthy heart and even longer life! This cookbook is for anyone who wants to follow a nutritious, delicious and low fat Mediterranean Diet Plan, whether they also want to lose weight or not. Enjoy the benefits of eating for optimum health, by following a low fat diet with 100+ Heart-Healthy, Low Fat Recipes using healthy, natural, wholesome, delicious ingredients.

The Easy Low Fat & Low Cholesterol Mediterranean Diet Recipe Cookbook features:

- Over 100 Easy Healthy Heart, Low Fat Recipes
- Low Cholesterol Diet Meal Plans for Weight Loss Dieting or Weight Maintenance Health Eating
- Everyday Mediterranean Diet Recipes for One or Two
- Satisfying Recipes for Family Dinners, Kids & Entertaining
- Options and Recipes for low fat Vegetarian Cooking
- Recipes that use healthy, delicious, naturally cholesterol-lowering whole foods and super foods.

Packed Full of Useful Information on Low Fat, Low Cholesterol & the Mediterranean Diet

The book also provides clarity and simple to understand information about:

- Cholesterol And The Different Types Of Cholesterol
- Fat And Cholesterol
- Eating For Lower Cholesterol
- The Heart-Healthy Mediterranean Diet Demystified
- Cholesterol Busting & Cholesterol Free SuperFoods.

Cooking for a Healthy Heart

If you are worried that adjusting your diet to support your cholesterol-lowering goals will be difficult or leave you feeling unsatisfied or deprived, think again. There are tempting and deliciously-good food recipes for Breakfast, Lunch and Dinner along with mouth-watering Desserts and scrumptious Bakes & Cakes.

You will find flavourful, cholesterol-lowering, healthy make-over recipes of:

- Mediterranean Diet Meals including *Baked Falafels Pittas with Tzatziki, Bellissima Beef Lasagne and Risotto Primavera*
- American Classics including *Cinnamon Apple Pie Pancakes, Quick Eggs Benedict, BBQ Chicken Sliders with Fruity Slaw and 'Hearty' Mac 'n' Cheese*
- Traditional British Pub-Food including *London Particular Soup, Shepherds Pie and 'Fish, Chips & Mushy Peas' with Tartare Sauce*
- World Flavours such as *Spicy Seed & Carrot Flatbreads, One-Pot Pilaf and Fragrant Chickpea, Pumpkin & Coconut Stew*
- Slow Cooker & CrockPot Specials such as *Boston Baked Beans, Chile Blanco and Lamb & Flageolet Bean Ragout*
- Delicious Desserts and Baking including *Strawberry & Rhubarb Vanilla Crumble, Ginger and Lemon & Blueberry Swirl Cheesecake.*

Resources include:

- several different two-week Menu Plans to help you get started
- advice on useful kitchen kit for healthy cooking
- heart-healthy store cupboard essentials
- stocking your fridge & freezer.

This is a practical, informative and helpful companion will work hand in hand with your plans to bring down your cholesterol.

This #1 Amazon Best Seller in Low Cholesterol Cooking is available as an eBook & Paperback

Watch a video preview of the recipes in this cookbook on Youtube @ https://youtu.be/F1z-XMF84qI

# Easy Low Fat & Low Cholesterol Healthy Brunch & Breakfast Eats Recipe Cookbook

Whether it's a quick, early bite to eat on a busy, weekday morning or a relaxed and leisurely brunch with the papers at the weekend, breakfast is often described as the most important meal of the day. Unfortunately, typical breakfast choices these days can be high in saturated and/or trans-fats, over-loaded with refined sugar, high in salt and low in dietary fibre.

However, it really doesn't have to be this way! Eating breakfast can be both delicious and healthy, especially as breakfast offers a great opportunity to increase your dietary intake of beta glucan. This cookbook will provide a wide variety of healthier breakfast and brunch dishes to savour and enjoy that are low in saturated fat, trans-fat, salt and refined sugar.

There are plenty of breakfast and brunch options from quick, easy, healthy breakfast dishes on-the-go on early-start mornings through to indulgent and sociable brunch meals for later, longer weekend mornings. There are recipes that you can prepare ahead and even ones that can the prepared overnight!

In this *Healthy Brunch & Breakfast Eats Recipe Cookbook*, you will find over 55 low fat & low cholesterol meal ideas including:

- Porridge & Soaked Overnight Oats including *Strawberry Cheesecake Overnight Oats*

- Breakfast Mushrooms including *Golden Mushroom Hash Browns*
- Breakfast Fruits including Peach, Raspberry & Pistachio Breakfast Crisp
- Love Your Heart' Super-Green Smoothies including Plum Crazy For Granola Green Smoothie
- Breakfast Salads including Tropical Fruit Breakfast Salad with Warm Granola Sprinkle
- Muesli & Granolas including Nutastic Seeded Muesli (Fruit-Free)
- Breakfast Bakes including Apple, Oat & Pumpkin Seed Scones
- Breakfast Eggs including Cheesy Eggs Florentine

Each recipe is low in saturated fat and many are rich in beta-glucan. There are lots of recipes that are also Vegetarian & Vegan.

In this cookbook, you'll find quick, easy healthy breakfast dishes perfect for busy weekday mornings as well as more indulgent, comforting recipes perfect for social weekend brunches. There are recipes that you can prepare ahead and even ones that cook overnight. This inspiring and exciting recipe collection is sure to become an essential part of your low-cholesterol kitchen.

Available as an eBook & Paperback

Watch a video preview of the recipes in this cookbook on Youtube @ https://youtu.be/ke9A11qaPcc

## Quick & Easy Low Calorie & Low Fat Desserts, Cakes & Bakes Diet Recipes Cookbook

This book features over 40 Recipes, including:

- Healthy Baking for Tempting Sweet Treats
- Delicious, Crumbly Diet Cookies that you won't believe are low fat
- Warming & Comforting (Low-Fat) Hot Puddings
- Heavenly-Healthy but Devilishly-Tasting Dessert Ideas
- Cute Diet Cupcakes & More-ishly Healthy Mini Bites
- Simply Scrumptious Low Fat Savoury Bakes & Breads

And they are all 200 Cals & under - and also low in both total fat and especially saturated fat!

All made from natural ingredients with no artificial sweeteners.

- Healthier Make-overs of Family Favourites
- Quick & Easy weekday recipes ready in 30 minutes or sooner, or
- Perfectly Portioned Puddings for 1 or 2, or
- Indulgent Sweet Treats that will help keep evening snacking at bay, or
- Healthier Cookies and Bakes to share with friends and colleagues or
- Elegant Parfaits and Trifles perfect for Entertaining

With each recipe showing the per-serving value for calories, total fat and saturated fat, you will find them all here.

With this healthy baking book you will be able to enjoy delicious recipes such as:

- Puddings & Desserts 150 Cals & Under such as *Spiced Plum & Honey Parfaits 144 cals, Pecan Streusel Stuffed Maple Peaches 120 cals and Slow Cooker Baked Apples 108 cals.*
- Puddings & Desserts 200 Cals & Under such as Blackberry Bakewell Sponge Puddings 158 cals, Tiramisu 199 cals and Mint Chocolate & Raspberry Pots 183 cals.
- Breads, Scones, Cookies & Biscuits such as Cranberry & Orange Scones 121 cals, Pecan, Maple & Banana Tea Bread 157 cals and Carrot & PB Oat Crumbles 91 cals.
- Cakes & Muffins such as Courgette & Orange Drizzle Cake 200 cals, Glazed Vanilla Lemon Teacakes 85 cals and Mini Cinnamon Doughnuts 122 cals.

This #1 Amazon Best Seller in Desserts is available as an eBook and paperback

## Bonus Two Day 5:2 Diet Plan FREE Giveaway

As a special Thank You to my readers, I have available an exclusive & free special bonus: FREE 1 Day Taster eBook, my complete and easy step-by-step guide to the 5:2 diet. Download your free copy here:

https://Free52DietRecipes.blogspot.co.uk

## Staying Connected

Please do also take a look at my author blog, MillyWhiteCooks.com.

As well as details on my full range of cookbooks, you will also find articles and helpful information on:

- Ingredients
- Cooking Techniques
- Equipment
- Health News
- Nutrition Information
- Special Offers

You can find me on social media too:

 MillyWhiteCooks.com

 facebook.com/MillyWhiteCooks

pinterest.com/MillyWhiteCooks · instagram.com/MillyWhiteCooks

twitter.com/MillyWhiteCooks · plus.google.com/+MillywhitecooksBooks/posts

# RECIPE INDEX

Printed in Great Britain
by Amazon

80693109R00040